FINDING
UNREASONABLE FAITH,
NO MATTER WHAT.

# CHOOSE

# Yes

*You are Loved!*

## Courtney Casper

# CONTENTS

# DEDICATION

To my husband, Tyler, who has stood by me, carried me, run next to me, forgiven me, loved me, laughed with me, defended me, encouraged me, and everything in-between. I love you; forever.

To my children. Lynley, I love how God made you nurturing and imaginative and brave. Callie, I love how God made you sensitive and loving and smart. Elaine, I love how God made you intuitive and caring and curly. Nolan, our tiniest boy, I love how God brought you into our family as the perfect missing puzzle piece, making our hearts whole and complete.

And to my mom, who has loved me, and fought for me to stay in the light, every day that I've been on this earth.

Lay all your
no's down at the
Saviors feet
& choose faith
— INSTEAD —

Courtney Casper

♡ ⎙ ✈

# INTRODUCTION

My own *yes* to God has been a twisty and broken road. But for every skinned knee, wrong turn, and shouted-at-the-top-of-my-lungs *no*, I'm still here. Because while in all my frail bit of humanity, the One who calls my name, keeps His promises. Promises of peace in heartbroken places, of redemption from deep and hidden shame, of strength beyond our own, and so much more.

These pages are the untangling of the beautiful mess that is living a human life, in the only way I know how, through letters and words. It's my anthem of *yes* to an unwavering faith, to a loving and knowing Father in Heaven, and *all* that he calls me to walk through.

I used to believe I was past His reach and love. Beyond His capacity to care or know.

But, I've found a *why* behind my *yes*. That *why* is complicated and deep and hard, but it keeps me stubbornly rooted in a *yes* to God, no matter how hard the wind blows. I need Him. I need His love. I need my children to know Him, and be known by Him. I need my family forever. I need light. I need hope. I need connection. I need help. I need a Savior.

Those are my *whys*. And when I want to quit faith, when I want to throw my tired hands in the air in defeat, when I want to stomp on everything until it's dust, I remember and feel them deep in my bones. They ground and keep me going for even just one more day. And one more. And one more.

My *why's* are now so ingrained in who I am, even on my absolute worst days, I still stand on whatever rooftop I can with tears in my tired eyes, scraped knees and aching heart, and *still* declare a *yes* to God, and His all.

What are your *whys?* Dig them up, uncover them, dust them off, and bring them back to life. Because *only* they will sustain you in the eye of a hurricane.

Consider this book a giant hug from me to you. I'm hugging you, but also I'm grabbing you by the shoulders, begging you to wake up to the **TRUTH** about who you are, and what you're here on this earth to be. Begging you to lay down all your *no's* at the Saviors feet, and **choose faith,** instead.

Raise your voice, open your heart, and declare your *own* anthem to God, of **yes.**

*Yes,* to the ebbs and flows.

*Yes,* to every narrow road.

*Yes* to faith, in the face of fear.

*Yes* to forgiveness, when covered in shame.

*Yes* to hope, even in doubt.

*Yes* to trust, when it's all unknown.

*Yes* to love, above all else.

*Yes* to showing up, again and again.

*Yes* to it *all,* in *unshakable faith.*

Look
Find
Choose

♡ ◯ ▽

# CHoose

## CHAPTER 1

Choosing *yes* is **brave**. Because those first *yeses* to faith are scary, found on uphill roads covered in fog. But it turns out, trudging through that fog is sacred ground. Every *yes* whispered or shouted or hoped for, burn who you once were to the ground, allowing a new self to grow from the sacred ashes. It's a treacherous and beautiful process, a gift.

I spent years fighting against those paths, "*No. No way. Faith is too hard. I don't deserve love. I can't trust God here. Why me? Why this? No. I can't.*"

Maybe you too have been saying a lot of *no's*. *No* to faith when storms of life rage. *No* to hope, *no* to love, *no* to forgiveness. Maybe you're on the fence about faith and what to believe at all. Maybe your heart is heavy, burdened with your current circumstances. *I've been there.* But this radical change that has taken place somewhere deep in my heart cannot be unraveled. And it all started, with one *yes.*

I am learning true conversion grows from a daily practice of faith in *every* uphill battle. *Looking* for reasons to believe. *Finding* light in the darkness. Choosing *yes*, every day, to every unknown, on every Red Sea Road that God calls us to walk. We say *yes*, and then *wait* for the Lord to reveal His plans, His love, and His grace. And He does.

Declaring *yes* to Him may feel unreasonable and big and brave.

**Because it is.**

I have a vivid memory of my daughter, Callie, she must've been 3 at the time, standing on the edge of our front step. Wearing a pink coat, lime green beanie, boots, and tightly holding onto as many things as she possibly could, including a fruit snack held between her tiny teeth.

The girl knew she could take only what she could carry out of the house. And she was going to make the most of that deal between me and her. What isn't seen in the photo, is the 8-minute back and forth power struggle between a very stubborn three-year-old and her already late mother. We battled on that day on how many things were too many to carry. I remember getting on my knees to be eye to eye with her near hysterical self, saying over and over, *"You have to choose what you want to bring; you can't bring it all. You can only bring what you can carry. You have to choose, either the stuffed moose, or the princess Sofia book. You can't bring them both; One or the other."*

Eventually she gathered every single thing she could possibly gather and walked out the door, into the already running minivan. But before she could wobbly step down that one step, I snapped a photo. Because it was a moment. It was something that has stuck with me.

We are making a choice, just like Cal.

We simply *cannot* carry it all, do it all, and be it all. Only what fits in your life, in your minutes, in your heart, is what fits. Maybe it's time to confront what is in your grip, and put some things down, so you can pick up some different things.

Choosing faith, is not something that can balance on top of our heads when our arms are full. We may be able to balance it there for a few minutes, but eventually, it *will* fall to the ground.

Choosing faith cannot be chosen last, because last, doesn't have room for anything. I know this, because I've been there. Carrying a million things that took up every single second of every single day, and when I desperately needed my faith, it wasn't there. It was left on the upper shelf in the cupboard that never gets opened, and when I *really* needed it, it was unusable.

Which left me in a world of hurt, making decisions I never would have made had I been choosing faith all along. I was hanging out in the darkness on the edge of spiritual cliffs, questioning all I had once believed.

Once I finally pivoted my eyes toward Jesus, I started putting down some things and picking up new things instead. My life shifted toward light when I stopped right where I was, and chose *yes* to faith.

I've been asked more times than I can count for a bulleted list to a thriving faith.

And believe me, I've tried to make a cute printable of any such thing.

But it doesn't exist until after *you*, in *your* unique circumstance and personality and ability, choose *yes* to faith, in action and obedience and sacrifice.

The list is simple, then. **You rediscover faith by choosing it.**

And the personal aftershock of that groundbreaking moment, is a million small moments after, that create a life lived with purpose and love and trust and God.

And it's everything, and *more*.

At the end some chapters, there may be an *"affirmation"* section. An affirmation is the process of coming to know, or coming to acknowledge something. While exploring different spiritual practices, many of which I'll share with you in this book, affirmations, or empowering borrowed thoughts, guided my heart on a journey of knowing and believing, **truth once again.**

What started as an attempt to change my way of thinking, turned into a practice of prayer.

These sections were created to inspire you as *you* personalize what you just read, opening the door to further insight and enlightenment for *you*, individually. Repeat them in your mind, write them on your heart, and come to know and believe, **truth**.

## AFFIRMATION:

As a child of God, you have the power within you to stop right where you are, today, and declare *yes* with a renewed faith that goes against all odds. No matter the circumstances or Goliaths standing in your way, *you* have the ability to put away all the reasons *no* seems like the common sense answer, and **choose yes** instead.

*You can do hard things.*

You can say *yes.*

**Declare it.**

And *live* it, every single day.

_____

_____

_____

_____

_____

_____

_____

_____

_____

_____

_____

_____

_____

Walk
YOUR
Red Sea
Road

Courtney Casper •••

♡ ▢ ◁

# Red Sea Road

## CHAPTER 2

There's a running joke in our family about how terrible I am with directions. How my mom got anywhere without a GPS in her hands at all times, is a mystery to me. Because while we've lived in this area more than a few years, I still use my GPS to get from home to, pretty much anywhere else. While I can finally get to Costco and Target on my own, I don't risk many other places without its confident robot voice keeping me on track and on time.

How nice would it be if we had an app called "God's Plan?" We could open it up each morning and see exactly how that day would play out. It'd have alternate routes when things were looking tough, timelines, and workarounds to every road block. Complete with an all knowing, confident voice to get us to each next step, as efficiently as possible.

In Exodus, we learn of the Israelite people fleeing Pharaoh. With Moses at the helm of the large group seeking asylum from their enslavers, many people were more than concerned when Moses led them to the edge of the Red Sea. Not to a bridge or boat to get over it, not to a path around it, but right to the very edge of it. Face-to-face, toe-to-toe, with its massive distance and unwavering waves crashing in and out. With an army at their backs, their future seemed bleak, at best.

At times our lives will look just as impossible as standing at the edge of the Red Sea.

We will even be *led* there, *guided* toward that sacred place, left alone to consider, *what now.*

God makes a way for Moses and the Israelites. He parts the actual waters of the Red Sea. Perhaps arguably one of the most well-known and stunning miracles in all of scripture.

**I'm coming to believe that God will part the waters in our lives, just the same.**

When we choose *yes*, it begins standing at the edge of a Red Sea Road. Toes in the sand, our faith and trust start to flourish when we take that first brave step, toward a miracle, a way through, an impossible road made possible by our Father in Heaven.

*What Red Sea Roads is God calling you toward today?*

Are you standing at the edge of the water, scared that maybe He won't be there to part them?

Are you frozen in fear, that perhaps you aren't cut out for *this* particular Red Sea Road?

Maybe this road isn't something you wanted, isn't something you expected, isn't something you can possibly imagine a happy ending to.

I've been there.

But here's the truth: **He will**. He *will* make a way. He will strengthen you, guide you, and love you through this. He will whisper to your weary heart the way you should go, and when you choose *yes* to His voice, trusting in His ways, you will start to become who He created you to be.

Each and every Red Sea Road is sacred ground. Name your struggles and setbacks and hard days what they *are,* an opportunity for God to work in even the tiniest details, so when He parts the sea, *you can name the miracles too.*

You are known. You are right where you should be. Take a deep breath, and trust that He *will* part even this, Red Sea.

_____

_____

_____

_____

_____

_____

_____

_____

_____

_____

_____

_____

_____

hold onto a
FAITH that
goes BEYOND
the LIMITS of
LOGIC.

Courtney Casper  ···

♡ ◯ ▽

# UNREASONABLE

## CHAPTER 3

Unreasonable: beyond the limits of acceptability or fairness.

When exploring my capacity for faith, I began to see the depths of the reality that the very existence of things like faith and trust and hope, meant the existence of seemingly unfair and illogical circumstances, too. Faith, in and of itself *is* **unreasonable**.

*"Believe in God; believe that he is, and that he created all things, both in heaven and in earth; believe that he has all wisdom, and all power, both in heaven and in earth; believe that man doth not comprehend all the things which the Lord can comprehend"* (Mosiah 4: 9, The Book of Mormon).

Can you lean in with unreasonable faith? Faith, against all odds? Faith, that defies logic? Faith, that lets go of what you don't know or understand, trusting that His ways are higher than yours?

and the
soul
felt its
worth.

♡ ◯ ▽

# GENEROSITY

## CHAPTER 4

Early in my journey back to faith, I realized recognizing God's power over my life was confined by what I believed He could do and be. When I began to *practice* believing in His power and love and redemption, I started to see it more and more. I started to see myself as part of His Kingdom. My generosity toward Him opened my eyes to someone beyond just a supreme being, but to a Father. **A God who saw me.**

Practicing generosity in faith may seem a little out of the box, but hear me out. *How often do we allow faith to lead the way when the path is easy, clear, and smooth sailing?* Probably fairly often. Because leaning into faith during times of ease, is just that, easy. It may even come second nature at some point.

*But what about when things aren't so easy? What about when logic is really loud? Can we be generous with our faith then?*

Peter, when called through the wind and waves, abandoned all human logic by stepping out onto the tossing sea. He was generous with his faith, and in his wild generosity, he experienced the miracle of Jesus's power. He swung his feet over the edge of the boat and responded with his *yes*, in action.

*So, what about us then? Can we open our hearts with a generous faith and hope, no matter what?*

I have, many times, been compelled to loosen the grip on my expectations, and allow faith and hope, to turn my hardened and very stubborn heart, to Jesus instead.

There is a page in my journal written in tight scribbled handwriting in black ink that pains me, even now, to read back. An honest and vulnerable prayer, surrendering to the very real hopelessness and faithlessness that felt so deeply rooted in my heart, I was sure my emptiness and fear had become permanent parts of me.

I was holding onto logic *so* tightly that everything I believed, hoped for, and had faith in, was slipping between my fingertips. All that made sense was *no, no, no.*

I felt protective and stingy with my heart. I felt unworthy of such things like happiness and peace. I wasn't sure they even existed.

That's when I discovered the power of generously trusting in, and hoping for, something beyond my own comprehension. Beyond myself, my fears, and doubts. Beyond any and all circumstance. There, I found an unreasonable faith with a brave and generous, *yes.*

When I stepped into the unknown, like Peter, at the faint call of my Savior into seemingly impossible territory, **He was there.** He was there in ways that I'd never known.

*Was it all smooth sailing?* Not even a little bit. In fact, it was really hard and required a commitment that began somewhere so deep, I couldn't even name it, speak it, or share it. It was between me and Jesus, and while I began to extend generosity in my trust, it did *not* happen overnight.

It happened slowly.

Like watching our tomato seedlings sprout next to the big kitchen window in March; Just when I am sure they'll never grow, the tiniest bit of green pokes out from the dark dirt.

So much work in our spiritual lives happens in the dark.

When my eyes saw no growth, no life, no hope--allowing faith to generously penetrate my heart *anyway*, took practice and intentionality that I'd never extended before.

Something happened in all my newfound unreasonableness; the more I chose to hope against all odds, and to trust when uncertainty screamed in my face, the more hope was at my fingertips, and the more trust became my anchor. Even when it made absolutely no sense.

It was a real-life miracle.

And I am not a special case. I am not some exception to the rule.

I am the rule.

Hope breeds hope. Generously trusting in God's power as He calls us out into the waves, actually creates a way for us to swing our feet over the edge of the boat, and onto the cold sea. Essentially, unreasonably trusting that somehow, He *will* part the Red Sea, enables His power to

PART THE RED SEAS in our lives. To crash through every stumbling block, every doubt, every painful and debilitating fear. To find us, no matter where we've holed ourselves up. It enables His power to heal every wound, heartache, regret, and hidden shame. Generously living a faithful life, allows God to fully step in, and saturate the dark places with His everlasting light.

I am committed to a newfound *yes* to *all* that God calls me to. And it's changing me from the inside out.

While listening to "O' Holy Night," the lyrics *"and the soul felt its worth"* settled in around me.

And the *soul felt its worth*.

**When was the last time your soul felt its worth?**

The world wants you to believe that you are just a body of flesh and bone, born to mindlessly march, see only logic, and do what makes sense. Drift with the current of whatever comes along.

Not so.

*"And now as I said concerning faith—faith is not to have a perfect knowledge of things; therefore if ye have faith ye hope for things which are not seen, which are true"* (Alma 32:21, The Book of Mormon).

Your generosity with God will change things in the dark, making room for you to flourish in the light.

As we walk our individual paths toward our Savior, He is endlessly generous with us! He has faith and hope in us, *always*. But until we can extend those things back to Him, I am learning we can't fully participate in His goodness.

May we abandon our doubts, shame, and fear, instead doing as Peter did: leading with our generous hope in things we can't see, know, or name, with faith to swing our scared feet over the edge and walk toward Jesus. May we firmly say *yes* to a wild faith, even here.

## AFFIRMATION:

I will begin to open my tight grip on things seen and generously trust in things unseen. I will open my heart and trust in a Lord and Savior who ***generously loves me.*** I am worthy of His love. I am His.

_____

_____

_____

_____

_____

_____

_____

_____

_____

_____

_____

_____

_____

♡ ▢ ▽

# CALLING OUT

## CHAPTER 5

On a beautiful trip to Hawaii, my family and I went on a private surfing adventure. We'd all surfed a little bit and were excited for the chance to be taught in a secret surf location. We boarded a small boat with our teachers, and were off toward the open ocean. After arriving at the bay, we were told to stay right in the middle of two underwater coral reefs. We couldn't see them, but were warned that they were very much there, and if we ventured too close, we would get pushed up against their sharp surfaces.

After gearing up, a few of us went out with our instructors. Paddling out was easy enough, we were going with the current I suppose, muscles still fresh, tan going strong, it was the perfect day.

Because we outnumbered the instructors, they took turns helping us surf. I was content to lie on my board and relax on the rolling sea, so I volunteered to keep doing *that*, while the boys caught their waves.

I laid my head down on the board for what felt like 38 seconds, but

I soon realized I was caught in a current and already very far from our group. Luckily, I'm not overly afraid of sharks, otherwise a panic attack surely would have ensued.

By this time, the instructors also noticed I was quite literally drifting off to sea, and I heard a faint yell from one of them. I'm still not sure what he said, but I did see him hop on his board and quickly paddle in my direction.

The second I realized I was drifting I started paddling of course, but the current was just too strong. For every stroke I paddled, the ocean sucked me out another board's length. My arms were tired, and I started to get a little (*okay, a lot*) nervous as to how the instructor was now going to get us *both* back to the boat.

He reached me and I tried to laugh off the fact that I was a rookie and let myself be sucked out to sea. He was out of breath and playing it cool too, but I could feel his sense of urgency to get us moving toward the boat, and fast. He tied my board to his with the ankle strap, we stopped the chit chat, and paddled as hard as we could.

With each paddle we made a little headway, and after what felt like forever, we made it back to the group.

Tyler, my husband, was less than chill about my little adventure, and I was embarrassed, making it all a greatly awkward reunion.

*"It's totally fine! I'm good! That was crazy!"* I told the group with false confidence. When everyone calmed down, the nice surfer boy, bless his heart, really wanted me to have that surfing experience, so he set me up for the last wave of the day.

I was already exhausted, but figured how bad could this end? I'll surf right to the boat and collapse onto solid-ish ground.

Let's do this.

He set me up for the oncoming wave, firmly reminding me to head straight forward (as if I could steer the giant board) away from the coral reef and pushed me off.

I paddled. *Don't hit the reef, don't hit the reef.* Lifted up to my hands. *Don't hit the reef...*To the crouch position, and then to standing! I was doing it! The grown woman who had drifted out to sea had some serious skills!

I surfed, all right. Straight into enemy territory, the coral reef where I was trying so hard *not* to end up.

According to my brother and husband, the local surfer next to them commentated on the whole event:

*"Look at her go...No! Not that way! Oh no. She's gonna crash...that hurt."*

I did crash. It did hurt.

The young surf instructor again came to my rescue and pulled me back to the boat. Bleeding, exhausted, and with no pride left, I climbed back onto the small boat and vowed never again.

I still have a nice little scar in the shape of the coral's thrashing claws on my back, as a souvenir.

Showing up with God, I'm learning, is much the same. Just because it may seem like the perfect adventure, complete with sunshine and a tan, does not mean there aren't going to be things that will not go as planned.

I used to think that choosing a life with God, meant that all my problems would vanish, or at the very least, be miraculously easier. This dangerously made my faith contingent on how easy life was, because, let's face it, life is not easy.

Turns out walking with God *still* has its ups and downs. Drifting, loss, and heartache are all possibilities, *if not guarantees*. Pain, exhaustion, and being stripped of pride are also strong possibilities, *if not guarantees*.

But no matter how far we drift, how banged up we get, how bruised our hearts, He will always paddle out and pull us back. He will tether us to Him when we call out and let our walls down enough, to acknowledge that we need His help.

And His saving arms are even more capable than any young surf instructor's.

There's also something to be said for where our focus is.

Looking back, I find it interesting that even with my laser-sharp focus on *not* crashing into the coral, that's right where I ended up.

Focusing on each fear, invites those fears to the party.

If you've declared *yes*, felt that first ray of light, and put forth the effort of calling to Him, *why let fear sit at this table? Why focus on the what ifs?*

I used to think my fears were the realest part about me, but now I know God's love is.

Have you drifted off to sea, into doubt or fear?

That's okay, because, with a *yes* to faith, **fear is the uninvited one, officially.**

## AFFIRMATION:

I will keep paddling, choosing *yes* to trust in His saving arms, and I will not let fear run my life. I know that no matter what, He'll always be right there.

_____

_____

_____

_____

_____

_____

_____

_____

_____

_____

_____

_____

_____

_____

_____

_____

♡ ◯ ▽

# *UNINVITED*

## CHAPTER 6

I am constantly reminded that our trust is such a key ingredient to a life with God. Trust that He'll be there, trust that we're allowed in His places, and trust that it's all going to be okay, no matter how unnerving choosing light in the darkness may feel at first.

It's like showing up to a party *uninvited.*

A few years ago, when we first moved to small town Basin City in the outskirts of eastern Washington, I heard through the grapevine about a Christmas party another woman was having. I didn't know her, wasn't sure where she lived, but I *was* semi-invited by someone *she'd* invited. I desperately wanted, scratch that, I *needed* friends. I was desperate enough to show up to that party, uninvited.

I made macaroni and cheese for the kids, reminded Tyler of bedtime, and headed in the general direction of her home in the dark. I saw the line of cars down the street when I approached her road, but not totally sure which house was hers, I began window peeping to figure it out. Not my finest moment, but certainly not my worst.

At last I found the house with the big front window bustling inside with women, crafts, and treats. Just your average grownup Christmas party. I sat in my cold car for too long, running through the scenario in my head. *Do I knock? Do I ring the doorbell? Is the one girl I know there?*

It was starting to snow, and after seriously considering diving into the bowl of caramel popcorn by myself, I eventually gave up trying to perfect my entrance. I was going to finally, just say *yes* to this Christmas party, invited or not.

I slowly and bravely poked my head in the door and was met by a group of small-talking, lovely women. They didn't mind that I was the newcomer and welcomed me to the table with open arms. I was sweating and smiling too big, but I felt part of them somehow. I was thankful I'd gotten out of the dark, cold car.

Some of those women have since become my closest friends; maybe even more like sisters.

Showing up with God is so much the same. Sometimes we know the general direction of where He is. Maybe we've heard through the grapevine, but the specifics are fuzzy.

Maybe, it seems like God's house is full of people who already know each other, the game plan, and even the secret passed-down-from-generation-to-generation, salsa recipe. Not only do they know how to do this faith thing, but they're already good at it. They have conviction and they're brave all of the time. Maybe their lives look easier than ours, therefore making faith easier to access. Maybe they seem like the types of people who have it all together and "deserve" to be there.

They're on this imaginary "list" that we've created in our heads, and as we hang out in the car, it just seems intimidating and vulnerable.

But here's the thing: if you stay hidden in the car while the snow piles up on your windshield, you won't get the secret salsa recipe. You won't experience the warm welcome. You won't know *Him*, the love, the redemption, the power, the *everything*.

Plus, that salsa has changed my life.

After the effort of showing up, that first awkward time, coming back gets easier. His house starts to feel like your own. You can show up any time of the day or night, and your commitment to that relationship becomes increasingly sweet as you navigate through different seasons of life. Quiet seasons. Loud ones. Seasons of change, big and small. You get through stuff together. You learn to rely on Him, and you see His goodness saturate your very regular life. You and God make a way together, and it's as full as it is life-giving. Through thick and thin, you are knit together in purpose and love.

Coming home to things like daily worship and faith, can feel overwhelming when you try to look at the whole picture at once. I used to think I had to be all or nothing in my commitment or conversion to God. Either I was wildly committed to Him every day, every minute, in everything, or it wasn't worth trying at all. Any misstep, and I was a total failure. That thinking is such a toxic mindset.

With each intentional step on the path back home to my faith, I'm learning who God truly is. We turn our hearts to Jesus by showing up in little spaces, little ways, *every day*. We aren't expected to have all the faith stuff figured out overnight. We aren't expected to have perfect trust and hope. We simply need to show up and be seen as we are, willing to pivot toward higher and holier ways.

It's a process that happens slowly, and over time. It rearranges your priorities, energy, and thoughts. It feels both freeing and scary. The refining process of letting go of certain habits, thought patterns, and doubts is sacred work. Give it time. Do it slowly. Listen closely. Feel the heartbeat of your life change, as you walk with God and let Him lead the way.

Choosing *yes* is a practice of repetition. Create the space for prayer and come back to it the next day. Open God's Word today, tomorrow, and every day after. Connect to Him in all seasons and circumstances.

Get out of the dark car, get your buns up to the door, and come on in. If you're feeling late to the party, no worries; there's no better time than right now to *show up anyway.*

Turns out, there is no guest list. There's room for us *all* in His presence.

## AFFIRMATION:

**I am here.** And wherever "here" is, *that's okay.* I am not forever broken or past hope. I may be feeling a little awkward with God, maybe I'm full on running in the opposite direction of Him. Maybe I've made a mess of things, wondering how to clean it all up. Maybe I'm stuck, stumbling, or wandering. Maybe I'm suffering, heartbroken, or simply just in a rut.

That is okay.

I am *OKAY.*

No, I am *more* than okay.

I AM LOVED, and *wanted, even here.*

_____

_____

_____

_____

_____

_____

_____

_____

_____

_____

_____

_____

Faith
hope &
trust
are all a
choice.

♡ ◯ ▽

# FIND

## CHAPTER 7

There is provision, protection, perspective, and *truth* with Jesus. But there is often a specific word within His promises: ***find***. *We can **find** our answers to our prayers. You will **find** the power to avoid deception.*

*You will **find** the power to stay on the straight and narrow path. You will **find** greater power to resist temptation . We can **find** spiritual nourishment and protection.* It seems we have to ***find*** Him to take part in all that a life with Him promises.

Sometimes our search will require great efforts and sacrifice. Especially when the whole faith thing feels bulky and awkward, when you're out of the habit of searching and finding, or when truth feels far-fetched or out of reach.

But here's the thing: we're *promised* when we ask, seek, and knock, we *will* find a loving and kind Savior on the other side of those efforts.

Coming home to the spiritual practice of *looking* for Jesus, I realized there was a sacrifice to be made. I needed time and space to find Him. I couldn't leave it up to *chance*. I couldn't wait around to see if I had it left over, or if it would magically fall into my lap. I couldn't wait to see if I wasn't too tired at the end of a day. I couldn't wait on anyone or anything to make this happen. It was up to **me,** no matter how tired, skeptical, or broken I felt.

Finding our Savior and receiving revelation is up to us, individually. We have to show up, ask questions, seek from every good place, and knock on His door.

The path toward our Savior has no shortcuts. It's simply one action after another, and another.

One of those critical acts of obedience in my own path back toward Jesus, was time spent in the scriptures.

I often get asked how I have the motivation to study my scriptures every day. To which I always reply, *"I don't!"* It's hard for me, just like everyone else. But somewhere along the line, I let go of the expectation that I had to be reading a certain amount of verses, pages, or even minutes a day. I just show up and try my best, *most* days. I open my heart, to whatever God pours out, and in each interruption or pause to help kids, or swap over the laundry, or run to preschool pickup, I keep my mind on those truths stirring within.

At first, I was tempted to skim and speed read through the scriptures. I wanted to get this scripture study business checked off for the day, and move on to the next thing. But I quickly learned a deep and impactful study of the scriptures required more than the speed-read approach. For me, it was going to take more than my typical halfhearted efforts.

I had to stop once in a while to ponder. Reread. Stop. Write. Which can make getting into the scriptures frustrating, add a few little kids to the mix and it can feel like an all-out impossibility. A straight up wrestling match between our best of intentions and, well, *everything else.*

However, I'm seeing now that perhaps that slow kind of trekking through each verse is actually something special. I started asking myself, *why did I just stop? What words stood out to me? Why is this resonating with me?* Recording my thoughts in a notebook, those small bites of scripture study have become invaluable to me. The Spirit speaks to me in those pauses and in the words that jump off the paper. And when I return to those sacred scribbles, I am taught even more about whatever God is trying to whisper to my soul.

I am beginning to refuse *anything* to rob me of those few precious minutes in my day. Most days, those intentions keep me coming back to the scriptures. Every day? No. But most days. And most days is a huge improvement from no days. We do our best, and that's enough.

Faith has been likened to a seed many times.

If I hold a sunflower seed in my hands, it cannot serve me by existing alone.

I used to expect my faith to serve *me.* Believing that surely it should carry me and enlighten me and be there in full bloom for me to enjoy right now, right away, and without fail. Jesus should be knocking on *my* door.

But the law of physics or gardening or whatever, do not allow a sunflower seed in my hands to be a sunflower. Until the seed is properly planted and watered and cared for, it cannot reach its full potential. I can wish for zero gravity, but guess what? My feet are still planted on the ground.

Faith doesn't *first* serve *us*. **We** *first* serve faith. We *first* plant that seed in our hearts, and do the work it takes to cultivate that seed, to water and care for it. We make the effort to grow faith, and then, eventually, **it grows**. It grows into something that *does* serve us in all the ways we're promised.

We probably all know the story of the woman at the well, but if not, here's the Courtney version ;)

She wakes up, and at the top of her to-do list that day is:

*Find water*

She assigns the kids a job to occupy them while she's away, gathers her water pot, slips on her sandals, and makes her way down the dusty road on foot, toward the well.

It's quiet out of the bustling house. She takes a deep breath, settling into the quiet on her way to water.

As she's there in the stillness, a man approaches. He sits down next to her.

*"When a Samaritan woman came to draw water, Jesus said to her, 'Will you give me a drink?'"*

This is a time where being a woman does not serve her often. Women's rights are not something marched or fought for yet. Her worth is tucked deep inside.

He speaks, and she's not sure what to make of Him or His words.

*"The Samaritan woman said to him, 'You are a Jew and I am a Samaritan woman. How can you ask me for a drink?' (For Jews do not associate with Samaritans.)"*

Christ responds gently, beckoning her to come unto Him.

*"Jesus answered her, "If you knew the gift of God and who it is that asks you for a drink, you would have asked him, and he would have given you living water"*

But she's not quite there yet. Still a bit disarmed that a Jewish man is communicating with her today at the well, she hesitantly draws nearer, but slowly.

*"'Sir,' the woman said, 'you have nothing to draw with and the well is deep. Where can you get this living water?'"*

And then, Jesus gives her the whole thing. The beginning to the rest of her life:

*"Jesus answered, 'Everyone who drinks this water will be thirsty again, but whoever drinks the water I give them will never thirst. Indeed, the water I give them will become in them a spring of water welling up to eternal life'"*

*"The woman said to him, 'Sir, give me this water so that I won't get thirsty and have to keep coming here to draw water'"*

She begins to want more, and her perspective is forever shifted *when she finds Him.*

While she doesn't yet know that this man is the Savior Himself, she is starting to ask questions and seek for answers. She begins to thirst for *Living Waters.*

*"The woman said, 'I know that Messiah' (called Christ) 'is coming. When he comes, he will explain everything to us.' Then Jesus declared, 'I, the one speaking to you—I am he.'(John 4:7-15, Christian Standard Version).*

*When was the last time you sat in silence at your Savior's feet?*

*When was the last time you thirsted and went looking for Living Waters?*

His living water is like rain to our dry ground. It breathes life into our souls and spreads light into the darkness. Living Water strengthens our weaknesses, growing our faith and trust and hope. So when the tough days come, we are more fully bound to a Savior who has been there and done *even this.*

Our *yes* to God often will start with something as simple as watering our faith, through daily interaction with His Word and prayer. These things, when placed at the tippy top of our priority list will be provision for our soul every single day.

I am on a mission to instill self-discipline in my kids, that looks like making their bed in the morning and brushing their teeth. Those things don't seem all that important today in the grand scheme of things, and if you ask them, they actually seem really dumb and not important at all. And yet developing the self-discipline to do those things, even if it's only out of obedience to avoid a negative consequence today, is still something. And in 6 months, even if they hate brushing their teeth, they will be happy they did it when they avoid the ever-dreaded cavities.

Finding Jesus takes self-discipline. It requires acts of obedience.

Studying the Word of God is a *choice.*

Praying is always a *choice.*

Worshiping on the Sabbath is a *choice.*

It's all a choice. Your faith, your hope, and your trust.

Staying at the well with Jesus that day, was a choice. She could have easily said *no* to that extra time spent there with Him.

But she didn't. She chose *yes,* and from those few minutes with Jesus her heart was changed.

There is no time like **today** to pivot, take one step, show up at the well, and see who shows up with you. I promise, He'll be there.

## AFFIRMATION:

I will rearrange my heart and mind to focus on what truly matters, creating time to connect with God through His word! I will declare my own committed *yes* to Jesus. I am worthy of each effort to come unto my Father. My spiritual health matters. I matter. I am loved.

_____

_____

_____

_____

_____

_____

YOU
- ARE -
IN THE
HANDS
OF GOD.

♡ ◯ ▽

# NEW

## CHAPTER 8

If I haven't already established this yet, I am a tangible and visual student. I need physical reminders of spiritual things. I need practices that daily turn this physical self toward things higher and holier. I choose faith on purpose, otherwise it doesn't get chosen often enough, or at all.

It was late fall, and I was determined to create a miracle moment with God. I was struggling with my current circumstances, and decided I could coordinate an event between me and Him, if I really went all out to do so.

I made a dramatic announcement to my husband that I was going to the river to have a spiritual awakening. I'd be back before dark.

He gave me a strange look, but knowing I am equally stubborn as I am anything else, kissed me as I walked out the door.

I drove straight to the river, choosing an area with no people. It was the golden hour before sunset, peaceful, and quiet. This was the spot, the perfect location for my own personal ground breaking, reality shaking, heavens parting, spiritual experience.

You know the kind.

You've sat in testimony meetings, heart aching a little after hearing such "wow!" spiritual experiences. Wondering why you haven't had something like that happen. Why you've never heard the voice of your Father directly. Why you've never had the ground shake beneath your feet or mind opened to eternal things.

Well, I was tired of feeling on the outskirts of those stories. I wanted something more, and this was the perfect time and place to make it happen.

So, I took what I'd learned online about curating an event and tweaked it a little to curate this spiritual experience.

I had my favorite Christian music playing in my car, with the windows down. I got out and sat on the very top of my silver Ford Escape, crisscross, palms open on my knees, and started to just... just...

Force the heavens to split the sky? Demand the presence of God? Micro-manage personal revelation?

I didn't give up easily either. I waited and waited and waited. I switched positions to my knees, to the ground, and eventually back to my driver seat. I read scriptures, hymns, and changed up the music.

It wasn't "working". And I was so upset about it.

I'd showed up where I thought He should be. I'd curated the perfect climate for His presence. My heart was in it. I was all in.

And then it started to get dark, my stomach was growling, and I'd promised the girls I would read another chapter of Little House on The Prairie before bed. So, I started the car, and drove away from my little corner of the river bank, home to my people.

The very next morning was the usual amounts of hectic. Kids were running late, I'd slept in, the baby was up 3 times the night before, and I stubbed my pinky toe so hard I was sure it was broken.

With my underlying low boil discouragement about the night before, I purposefully moved my scriptures from off the kitchen table, without reading them. A true grownup act of defiance. Aka: a temper tantrum. *If God wasn't going to show up when I went to great efforts to reach Him, why would He show up at my kitchen table?*

*No. No. No.*

Despite the morning's best efforts, I was 7 minutes early to preschool drop off, and I could feel the tears just waiting to spill out. Why? I couldn't even tell you. But they were there and I was so angry and sad and confused and hurt and, it was raining. Because, of course it was raining.

I always carry a tiny set of scriptures in the center console of my car. I knew exactly where they were from the hours before at the river, where they'd proven unsuccessful to produce a miracle.

I started to think about them. Their size, color, the little wonky flower drawn in the front cover by Lynley. I couldn't stop my brain from dwelling on them.

In a fit of exasperation, I popped open the console and grabbed the miniature Book of Mormon. Fanned its pages, and then opened them up to a random verse and read.

You were waiting for the groundbreaking verse of scripture that altered my entire life, huh?

Nope. I couldn't even tell you what it was.

But. As I sat in my car, in my red and white striped pajamas and slippers, I felt like the grinch. My heart started to expand from its shriveled and bruised and disappointed state.

Elaine opened the automatic door, jumped out of the car, happily bounced through the preschool doors, and I felt... *happy, at peace, warm, loved, known, and heard.*

So often we beg and wish and demand spiritual experiences, personal revelation, guidance, comfort, or answers to show up pre-packaged up on our doorstep. The bigger the box, the better. The more dramatic the event, the better told from pulpits. The more intriguing and detailed and "wow", the more valid and powerful.

*I'm learning what hyped up nonsense this way of thinking is.*

Sure, I've had profound personal moments with God, but usually they come in the small moments of reaching. In showing up in the mix of hectic mornings with a willing and needy heart for His presence.

Creating space for connection and stillness and God is only as good as our ability to bring those things with us, *everywhere we are.* Because while Red Sea miracles exist, I'm learning they aren't reserved for the gallant and heroic. They're for you and me, and they look a lot more like every day battles through the trenches of life.

My mom and little brother Jacob have been trudging through the trenches of cancer for more than 5 years. I have watched them both, in different ways, move through days like they're walking in wet cement. One heavy step after another, refusing to remain stuck in its ever-solidifying ground. Leaning on and pushing toward a *yes* to all that God calls them to, with their own unreasonable faith. *Do they wish for a Red Sea miracle? A blind gaining sight, get-up-and-walk, moment?*

**Yes. We all do. Every day.**

*Do miracles still exist in the trenches? Are they **just as** powerful and moving and connecting?*

**Yes. They do. They are.**

*So, why then is it so hard to see the fruits of our efforts toward faith, day to day? Why do we fixate on the big and bold evidence of His presence in our lives, rushing through the small and simple? Why not stand at a pulpit in church bearing **just as** powerful witness to the reality that God is with you in the rainy preschool drop off?*

There will be times you feel aimless, stuck, lost, or unsure of where you belong or what you should be doing. Perhaps, you are in a new place in life, standing in all new circumstances. I'm learning there is everything we need, found right where we stand. *In our small daily efforts and aching open hearts and even fragile yeses.*

**"Know ye not that ye are in the hands of God?"** (*Mormon 5:23, The Book of Mormon*)

This short verse of scripture has changed the way I see my life.

*Knowing* that I am in the hands of my Father, in *every* new season and *every* new circumstance, changes the game. There is no need for angels to show their faces, or brilliant stories of lightning bolt revelation. Because over every day, *He is here.* Your moments of stillness at the kitchen counter are sacred ground. Your two-verse scripture study is *enough* to feel His presence. The prayer in your heart is heard and known. The small and quiet whisperings from the Spirit are profound revelation. And the wet cement of trial, shapes you around *His miracles, His love, and His presence.*

_____

_____

_____

_____

_____

_____

_____

_____

_____

_____

_____

_____

_____

_____

_____

_____

_____

_____

_____

_____

_____

_____

_____

_____

_____

_____

_____

offer god
more than your
HIGHLIGHT ROLL.

# PRAYER

## CHAPTER 9

Our kids have been praying for cures and healings for more than five years. Just last night Callie bowed her head, closed her eyes, and prayed that her uncle Jake's cancer would be healed.

I have a hard time keeping my composure during those prayers. There's something about the innocence and vulnerability that children possess that we somehow lose along the way. My heart aches in longing for that kind of confidence in a God who will move mountains.

She doesn't fight the desires that come to her heart. She simply lays it all on the table with her Heavenly Parents when she connects to Them in prayer. She desires her uncle to be healed. She doesn't take into account recent scans or logic or become discouraged in any way. She is an open vessel in prayer, and I am envious of that kind of courageous desire.

Desiring to remain hidden from God keeps me stuck in patterns of halfhearted, half mumbled prayers. I hide my desires, and any struggle that I can possibly manage *myself.* Unlike my innocent children, I show up in prayer like a curated Instagram feed.

The *"Prayer Highlight Roll."*

That's what I call it.

A collection of short, happy captions along with categorized life moments.

It's no wonder I don't feel connected to Him in that space.

Small talk with God is no different than small talk with the grocery store checker, it's pleasant, but not meaningful.

God becomes like an old acquaintance that is still in my Instagram following. I allow Him to peek into the best parts of my days while I get to peek into His, and then I scroll on.

I have spent a lifetime hiding the behind-the-scenes from my Heavenly Parents. Convinced they don't have the time to sift through it with me, unworthy of such connection. For too long I have believed that prayer is a painful admission of all the ways I am failing, a short and awkward exchange between me and the empty space around me.

It's so hard to put into words all the ways my believed un-lovability has distanced me from God. It's painful. Like a child who has run away from home. Always wishing to return, but unsure how to show up. Because showing up is admitting that you missed home in the first place, that you were wrong, that you are scared, alone, and hurting. It's a blow to the ego to admit that home never disowned *you*, but that *you* disowned home. That home never stopped loving you, but you turned your back on that love. It's a tough pill to swallow, and it feels like stepping off a plane in a new country. Everything looks, feels, and sounds different.

Part of retraining yourself to believe you're worthy of love requires an amount of childlike vulnerability.

Relearning how to pray started on paper for me. My favorite pastime of doodling turned to doodling passages of scripture first. Over and over I would write the promises of God over myself.

*"I can do all things through Christ who strengthens me!"*

*"Doubt not, just believe in Christ."*

I used to think prayer was only true prayer if the words were thought up on the spot, different each time. If my prayer wasn't said with closed eyes and folded arms, spontaneously formed, it wasn't really prayer at all.

But the silent and closed eyes kind of praying doesn't always "work" for me. I often get fidgety, distracted, uncomfortable, and at a loss for words.

After 30 something years of praying the same way, or not all, I needed a change of pace. I needed a new perspective.

My doodles became more and more of a lifeline to me when the darkness loomed close by. Day after day, I began to realize that this "doodling" was something more, that these words repeated in my heart and mind again and again were more than just repetitive words, they were prayer in every sense of the word.

So, I bought a Moleskin notebook and began a daily practice of writing my prayers down on paper. I first focused on the honest truth, the desires, the weaknesses, and everything in-between. Simply, *"I am struggling to know that I'm really loved. I'm overwhelmed with my life. I'm worried about this child. I am struggling in my marriage. I feel regret so big. I am tired."*

I don't write, *"I'm worried about this child, and I'm sorry I don't have the answers."*

Or, *"I'm overwhelmed with my life, I really need to stop doing that."*

I start by pouring out the real stuff with a superhuman amount of vulnerability, and trust that my Heavenly Parents are going to be there. That they aren't going to chuckle and roll their eyes, but instead hold it all with me, their imperfect daughter, in patience and love.

I'm learning it's okay to borrow our prayers.

We can borrow them from scripture, others, books, hymns, or any place that offers enlightenment and connection to God. So many of our ordinance prayers are written down and read, said exactly the same each time. Does that discount their importance, weight, or worth? No, of course not! It's actually one of the ways Jesus instructs us to pray in the Bible, and carries into important covenants to this day.

There is room for all kinds of prayer in your life. Spoken ones, written ones, borrowed or formed on the spot.

Callie recently brought home two pieces of artwork from school. Black pieces of paper as big as her, she had drawn a Frankenstein with pastels on one sheet, and a family of bats on the other. The one looked much more formal than the other, and I asked her if she had some help with the Frankenstein drawing. She told me that drawing was a "directed draw" for the whole class. Their teacher directed each shape and detail, so they could create artwork that was above their skill level otherwise.

I wasn't any less in love with the directed draw artwork than the wonky little family of bats.

She was beaming proudly of both papers, and while Halloween has long since passed, they hang on our art wall still to this day.

Callie is learning about art and pastels and the directed draw expanded her abilities and perspective, through the guidance of a teacher. Starting with a Frankenstein shaped head, ending in the tiny screw bolts and zigzag scar, she made art beyond her capacity.

Choosing *yes* to prayer is vital to your faith. I borrowed prayers and spoke them over my life again and again, holding onto those truths when I needed them most. Directed by the scriptures, I found a true connection to God through those sacred doodles. Written prayer has become a vital practice in my spiritual life.

*Why is prayer life-giving and absolutely vital in your yes to faith?*

I like to think we are all carrying a backpack. Often, it's filled to the brim with rocks--our heavy baggage and burdens. We carry around this backpack day in and day out, continuing to add to it with each regret, fear, and hurt. Prayer, for me, is the spiritual practice of taking off and unpacking it all, and slowly, one by one, pulling out each rock and laying it at Christ's feet.

*"Come unto me, all ye that labour and are heavy laden, and I will give you rest. Take my yoke upon you and learn of me; for I am meek and lowly in heart: and ye shall find rest unto your souls. For my yoke is easy, and my burden is light"* (Matthew 11:28-30, King James Version).

He doesn't say, *"Come unto me all that have life figured out, all that feel perfectly at peace, loved, and whole."*

He says, *"Come unto me all those who labor and are heavy laden."*

He doesn't say, *"Come unto me those who know everything about me."* He begs us to come and *learn.*

He doesn't say, *"Come unto me all of you who are well rested and filled with light."*

He says, *"Come unto me and find rest, light, and love."*

Vulnerable and meaningful prayer, sifting through all the stones, rocks, and boulders, laying them down one by one with no excuses or already planned out solutions, began a process of truly feeling and knowing a love, that surpassed anything I could ever imagine.

**Prayer is a practice.**

It's a practice in releasing all our true desires, even when those desires are cures for cancer even still, or peace in the storm. Even if it's for strength to continue walking through a mess you made yourself. It's a practice that goes beyond the "highlight reel" allowing us to fully experience the constant and tangible connection to Heavenly Parents, who are there for it *all.*

There to ease burdens and offer rest to our souls.

There to strengthen, comfort, and LOVE.

There to heal brokenness so big and wide we're sure it can't be done.

Until it *is* done.

I used to think I was unworthy to be one of the lucky few who had a connection with God through prayer, but I have learned, none of us are the exception to the truth and rule: Prayers are heard, we are known, and loved.

## AFFIRMATION:

My prayers uttered while driving, prayers offered in dark closets with heavy hearts and stinging tears, prayers that are written or yelled or spoken in the dead of night, are *all* heard. I will consistently choose *yes* to prayer, opening the door to a deeper and braver *yes* to God. I am known. I am heard. *I am loved.*

_____

_____

_____

_____

_____

_____

_____

_____

_____

# WHY

## CHAPTER 10

I was 11 when my parents explained to my three younger brothers and I that they were getting divorced. Those moments on the couch as a young girl were devastating, and are etched into who I am today. The years that followed were transforming in many ways. Though no one fully abandoned me, I felt abandoned by a family that no longer existed. Life as I knew it changed. I didn't have the option to say *yes* or *no* to my life circumstances at 11. They were what they were. And they were hard.

I wondered how God could let this horrible thing happen to my little brothers and me. I begged Him to change it all, turn back time and change my parents' minds. I wanted Him to take me back to southern Florida when everything felt whole, happy, and warm. For decades, I struggled to understand a God who would allow something so terrible to happen to our family.

In different seasons, the sting of divorce has shaken me in different ways. But I always clung to the things I learned in Primary: I was a child of God; and He had sent me *here*. He would lead, guide, and walk beside me and help me find my way. Looking back, I want to hug my younger self and tell her that she will be okay. In fact, she'll be better than okay, she will be exactly who God created her to be.

Standing where I am today, I can see that even during those moments, I was in God's hands all along.

I've often thought about Hagar in the Old Testament. As an Egyptian slave, I suppose she didn't carry with her elaborate or intricate plans for her humble life, but surely an unwanted marriage wasn't her first choice. In fact, the Bible tells us that when she learned she was pregnant, she struggled deeply with Sarai. The feelings were unfortunately mutual.

It turns out, life is twisty and not always what we expect it will be, all throughout the history of time.

Fourteen years after the birth of Hagar's precious son, Ishmael, Sara (formally Sarai) bears her own promised son, Isaac. Soon after his birth, Sarah demanded to eliminate the threat to her son once and for all, banishing Hagar and Ishmael to the wilderness.

Hagar had received direct revelation from God to endure her days as a slave, even to enter into the unwanted marriage and have a child. She mothered and loved Ishmael well, and stayed close to the Lord. Why then be cast out, left to starve and die in the wilderness? Why walk this heart wrenching road?

When things went from bad to unbearable, Hagar walked a distance from her dehydrated and starving child because she simply could not bear to watch him die. *"While she sat at a distance, she wept loudly"* (*Genesis 21:16, Christian Standard Version*).

Have you ever been there? Completely out of options, not even sure where you went wrong in the first place? In desperate need of the Lord, but unsure if He even sees or hears you?

Hagar *is* heard. An angel calls to her *"Fear not, for God hath heard the voice of the lad where he is. Arise, lift up the lad, and hold him in thine hand; for I will make him a great nation. And God opened her eyes and she saw a well of water; and she went, and filled the bottle with water, and gave the lad drink. And God was with the lad; and he grew, and dwelt in the wilderness"* (*Genesis 21:17-21, King James Version*).

The story of Hagar and Ishmael is a complicated one, who's life isn't at the end of their days? We have the privilege of seeing her life from start to finish, in multiple translations, with endless amounts of speculation. But what if we could put all that aside, and see Hagar in this moment of her life, and nothing else? Can we humanize this sacred and profound moment of despair for Hagar? Can we see, that even in our *own* twisty and sacred and profound moments, when we beg and cry out WHY to God, that He *will* see *us* and deliver *us*, too?

*Why*, when it seems we're doing things right, do bad things still happen? *Why* miscarriage? *Why* infertility? *Why* addiction? Infidelity? Anxiety? *Why* do good, God-fearing people get cancer? *Why* so much grief and suffering?

I have no answer for us. In fact, asking the heaven's *"why me," "why them," "why this," "why now"* never gets me any answers that feel comforting or healing. Those kinds of questions only lead me to things like resentment, discontent, and frustration in small whispers from the Adversary. I'm learning to ask a different question in the face of these kind of uphill seasons.

I was recently in a meeting with a man, whom I love and trust as an ecclesiastical leader. He asked how I was doing, and I felt tears instantly come to my tired eyes. *I was okay.* The months prior had been a tailor-made kind of intense; Fighting demons that I'd never faced before with my mental health. I was beginning to come out on the other side, and this simple question brought it all to the surface once again. As I shared with him some of the more tender moments I had had over the prior months, he sat in silence, tears now filling his eyes as well. When I finished talking, we sat in the quiet for a few moments more. He then asked if I had ever wondered *why* God allowed these stumbling blocks to make their way into my life. Of course, I had! Even sitting there, I was still trying to solve for *"why"* in my heart and mind.

He challenged me to go ahead and wonder with God why difficult things happen, but in a different light. *What am I learning? Where are His tender mercies here? How can I draw closer to Him through this season? What can be strengthened? How is this pushing my roots of faith deeper, drawing me closer to my Savior?* **Why?**

This shifted something in my heart so suddenly, it was like truth instantly replaced doubt that my Heavenly Parents were aware of me in this particular storm. I began to take inventory of what I had learned, how I had drawn closer to Jesus, and what spiritual muscles were indeed strengthened. I saw tender mercies and miracles that accompanied even the most agonizing days. It was a paradigm shift of sorts, reassuring my weary heart that I was known, all along.

In Hagar's case, we never learn a logical common-sense reason as to *why* she was called to suffer so much. We simply read that in her desperate need, God hears her cry and saves her and her son's life. I imagine leading her to a renewed commitment to rely on the Lord following their deliverance.

Maybe seeking deliverance is designed to be uncomfortable and trying, so that when we receive it, we can more fully appreciate His hand in our lives.

"I am a child of God, and he has sent me *here*" ("*I Am a Child of God,*" *Children's Songbook*).

I used to wish for different circumstances. I wanted less suffering for those I loved. Fewer tragedies. No more mishaps and uphill-both-ways seasons of life. I used to believe that the suffering must be a momentary lapse in God's will, a blind spot. And most definitely, I believed it was unreasonable to ask *anyone* to have faith during God's "blind spot" moments.

I'm learning that is not even close to the truth.

We wish, and beg, and ache for something, *anything,* other than what is right in front of us. Convinced that surely *this* season of life isn't part of God's will, and we can only find happiness somewhere *else.* "Over there" is where true peace, purpose, and sunshine reside.

Jesus offered *presence* with those He interacted with in His mortal ministry. He met them where they were, not rushing them off to different places. He met Moses in his self-doubt. He came to Peter, when he was knee-deep in the life of a fisherman. He met the blind in their lack of sight. He met Mary and Martha in their grief. He met the woman at the well in her thirst for something more.

He meets us, just the same, right where we are *in* our individual seasons. And when He shows up, He doesn't chastise us for not being somewhere else. He doesn't scrunch his eyebrows and shame us, even if we've been saying *no* to faith or hope or charity. He is love. He is grace. He is **here,** and through Him, peace and happiness can be found, even in the middle of a hurricane. God can be found, even right *here;* When we look for Him, His goodness, His protection, and His love. We will more fully see and understand, His timing and His will, when we prayerfully ask the right questions.

Coming to your Savior, during whatever season you're in, requires soul work. It requires something beyond reasonability. Trusting that God is within reach, during the impossible, takes a faith equal to Peter when he walked on water. Equal to Moses', as he split the Red Sea. Divorce or sickness, sin, and everything in-between, we are never abandoned in any of it. He is here.

## AFFIRMATION:

I will dig deep and find the true reasons "why" I am *here*, trusting that no matter what, I am in the hands of my Father. Trusting no matter how dire my circumstances may look in this moment, God is right here with me. I will shout or whisper or hope for a *yes*, to all that He calls me to, in love.

_____

_____

_____

Courtney Casper ...

♡ ◯ ⊽

# QUESTIONS

## CHAPTER 11

I'm learning to pay attention to my questions.

I hated asking questions as a kid in school. I didn't want to look like I didn't know what I was doing or what was being taught. I didn't like drawing attention to my lack of answers, and so I'd sweat it out in my chair until I could put the pieces together on my own.

Which, as you might have guessed, led to a lot of sub-par grades.

As a new mom, before leaving the hospital with my 5lb 2oz baby girl, I had a zillion questions. At the last second, husband off to get the car, I frantically bombarded my poor nurse with every one of them. I didn't care how dumb I looked at 19, with this brand-new baby strapped into a car seat that seemed way too big for her.

Everything suddenly became real. I remember thinking, *How are they letting me out of here with her?! Don't they know I have no idea how to keep her alive?*

The gentle and kind nurse didn't ignore my frightened tears. She held space for them. And then she held *me*. She hugged me and answered all my questions in one sentence: *"You're her mom, and you will be a great one."*

I held onto her promise during the late nights when I didn't know why she was crying, *again.* During the painful nursing sessions, and through every other hard new mom moment too. And if I'm honest, I'm still holding onto that promise today.

I'd blurted out the scary questions of my heart to that nice nurse against my usual judgment of holding them all in, for fear of looking unprepared, incapable, or naive. And in return, I received the exact words I needed, time and time again.

I find solace in the practice of simply *letting my questions speak.* Breathing life into deeply personal questions can be a little scary. Allowing them to exist outside of myself, often feels vulnerable and raw.

But shoving all our questions down, pretending they don't exist, or trying to put all the pieces together ourselves is exhausting. It's tiring to constantly put on a front that we have all the answers, and do life on our own.

Letting pride lead the way, trying to power through life in our own strength, in our own way, and by our own plans, is really hard and dark and lonely. It's choosing *no* to God's promises. *Sure* promises, that *all* who come unto Him will be strengthened, comforted, redeemed, and led. Even us questioners.

Another amazing woman throughout scripture is Sariah. Her story of faith and trust resonate so deeply in my heart. If there was ever someone who was like you or me, it's her.

If you're not familiar with her story, here's another Courtney version for ya ;):

Sariah was wife to Lehi, a prophet. She had five sons. She raised them well, growing them from little boys into capable and powerful men. Together her and her husband taught them the ways of the Lord, and over the years they became a tight family unit.

These facts lead me to believe that Sariah was woman well acquainted with all the things. Joy and discouragement, long days, and sleepless nights. A woman who found herself on her knees in prayer often, in all circumstances. A powerful woman, just like you and me. A woman of God.

When her husband received visions and revelations from the Lord to uproot their entire lives for the wilderness, far from the wicked city of Jerusalem, she faithfully followed. *Yes.* She folded the linens and prepared the food, thinking of each family member, carefully tucking things into small bags and pouches.

Did she have questions about this call to action from God? Did she wonder where, how, and why? Did she yearn for more knowledge, more answers? Did she wonder why she didn't also receive a vision from her Father in Heaven? Did she ache for the home she had created and cultivated? Did she cry into her pillow at night when two of her sons struggled with this family decision? Did she tenderly pray on their behalf?

Regardless, they packed up their lives and walked into the wilderness.

Talk about faith in the face of a million unknowns.

A few days into their journey, Lehi received the direction from God that the boys were to return to Jerusalem to get the plates of brass, from the hard-hearted King Laban. They held precious truths and genealogy, and would not be easy to retrieve.

What did Sariah think about this? She knew it would be a dangerous mission, and there would be no way to communicate with her sons. It would be a goodbye without any sure bet of a happy reunion.

Sariah, with deep faith and devotion to God, packed up her sons, and sent them back to the wicked city, to get the plates.

Did her heart ache and wish for them to come home safely? Did she worry endlessly and pace back and forth? Did she pray and beg for comfort and safety?

With a shaky and fragile *yes* to God, she had done exactly what He asked. She stood on a straight and narrow path she never imagined, and then struggled to stay there.

*"For she had supposed that we had perished in the wilderness,"* (1 Nephi 5:2, The Book of Mormon).

Sariah questioned her husband's visions, she questioned God's plan for their lives, she mourned the loss of her children, her home, and her life as she knew it.

In this tender moment, God doesn't smite her down. He doesn't come down with an iron fist in response to her questions, her despair, her moment of hopelessness, or maybe even anger. And in return, she doesn't pack up and leave, throwing all her *yeses* to faith and trust to the wind. She questions **and** holds on. She allows her feelings to be felt, her questions to be spoken, and then she holds on and waits for God to break through as promised.

*"And it came to pass that after we had come down into the wilderness unto our father, behold, he was filled with joy, and also my mother, Sariah, was exceedingly glad, for she truly had mourned because of us,"* (1 Nephi 5:1, *The Book of Mormon*).

Joy after mourning.

Questions spoken and held and answered.

A newfound *yes* to faith and God's *all*, a new Sariah born through the fire of trial.

*"And she spake, saying:* **Now I know of a surety***,"* (1 Nephi 5:8, *The Book of Mormon*).

Are we so different from Sariah?

The promise of unconditional love and a deeper *yes* to faith after each fiery trial, cannot be broken by any question, any fear, or any doubt.

That is, if we choose to speak those tender questions in the presence of someone who actually has the answers. In things that really matter, Google is not your friend. How many of us have seen the 4am hour by the glow of our phones, and the endless Google pages and forums of information that you now wished you never knew? I'm raising my hand here.

Asking the nameless and faceless internet questions of deep and personal value is dangerous ground.

If you're child has pink eye (which mine currently does, so, that's fun.) turning to Google will yield you some interesting home treatments, but most will say "consult your doctor." Because, well, they're your kids' doctor, they're trained for this. They can give you the answers, the eye drops, and maybe the best gift of all, peace of mind, that despite what Google might say, your child will be A-okay, after all.

Why then, do we sometimes meander in places with our deep and personal and faithful questions, that simply will never hold any answers?

Again, I'm raising my hand here before anyone else. Because I've done it. I do it.

But I'm slowly learning that giving life to questions and even doubts and fears, in the presence of God, Jesus, in places with their light, make *all* the difference. I get answers. I get revelation. I come to know of a surety.

Raise your hand with all those questions—there's no judgment here. In fact, with God, every question can become sacred ground! It is a connecting point between you and Him, that will open the doors to profound personal revelation.

*"And he said unto me, my grace is sufficient for thee:* **for my strength is made perfect in weakness.** *Most gladly therefore will I rather glory in my infirmities that the power of Christ may rest upon me"* (*2 Corinthians 12:9, English Standard Version*).

His *strength* is made perfect in *weakness, in* your questions, and doubts, and struggles. His strength isn't exclusively a gift to the perfectly-faithful. It's a gift for us *all*. The middle grounders, the everyday completers. The average, constantly figuring it out, back and forth-ers.

If you can get brave and ask *Him* all those questions, His power dismantles us in the best way.

*"I will glory in my infirmities, that the power of Christ may rest upon me."*

Why glory in our infirmities? Because *through* them, we get to taste of the ultimate power of our Savior Jesus Christ. We get to *know* of a *surety*.

All is never lost, and you, my friend, are LOVED.

## AFFIRMATION:

I will choose *yes* to trust, to His promises, and to His love. I will let my questions speak in the presence of my Father in Heaven. I will embrace my weaknesses and allow them to become strong through the power of the Atonement. I will come unto my Savior, where I am, and He will be there with open arms.

---
---
---
---
---
---
---
---
---

_____

_____

_____

_____

_____

_____

_____

_____

_____

_____

_____

_____

_____

_____

_____

_____

_____

_____

_____

_____

_____

_____

_____

_____

_____

_____

_____

_____

_____

God consecrates our HARD moments when we WAIT on HIM in PATIENCE.

♡ ⃞ ⃗

# BiTTer & SWEET

## CHAPTER 12

Today has been a truly beautiful day. The sun is setting in the pink and orange sky. The air is so still and warm; I can't even feel it on my skin. Tyler, and our oldest daughter, Lynley, are out changing water on the growing wheat field. Two happy and healthy little girls are jumping on the trampoline. The squeezy baby boy is bouncing on my lap. It's a picturesque evening on our small piece of ground under our little patch of sky.  I can recognize the simple beauty of this regular Sunday night *only* because I've known dark, miserable, and fear-filled ones. I've felt the fog of uncertainty and the smothering arms of regret. I've been consumed by hopelessness, and desperate for deliverance.

The months that three of our children fought whooping cough ripped me from the light and safety of hope. I begged and pleaded with God to take this mountain away from my children, to make the coughing stop, to heal us totally and completely and now. *That didn't happen.* My two-month-old baby turned blue in my arms over and over again, as he coughed violently, fighting for air, for weeks. My older kids spent their entire summer vacation on the couch, lethargic and ill. My mental anguish peaked when I cried to my husband that I just couldn't do it anymore. I fought terrible thoughts that called me into total darkness.

I wanted to surrender, but not to the will of God. I wanted so badly to surrender to the darkness of depression and anxiety. I wasn't sure that I could go another day in that storm. My faith was paper thin and my hope was giving way to hopelessness with every passing moment.

I am blessed with an incredible support system. With one whisper of this raging storm, I had a friend by my side, holding my sick baby while I cried on her couch. I had a friend in my kitchen making cookies with my kids, who were desperate for a sense of normalcy that I just couldn't give. I had my mom on a plane the next day to fold laundry and hold us together while I tried to put *me* back together. I had a mother-in-law in our home holding down the fort so that I could rest and, just not be alone.

My husband was the one who made the appointment with a women's mental health specialist, the wonderful doctor who would change my days with a simple medication. Getting me through the endless coughing spells without my anxiety and depression crippling me. I had an army of internet friends whom I'd never met praying for us, by name, mightily working miracles in our home. These people, who fight their own battles every day, will never know how their prayers buoyed me up, and kept me in the light, when I so badly wanted to run away from it *all*. (*Thank you from the bottom of my heart.*)

Months later, my sweet kids are still coughing and not totally better, but I'm seeing the tender mercies that have been over us all along.

I'm seeing the miracles and protection poured into our lives, even in the middle of a very real to me, hurricane of hard. I'm seeing the deep foundation of faith that even a round of whooping cough couldn't destroy, maybe the biggest miracle of them all.

Total darkness cannot exist where even a tiny amount of light is present. But, likewise, we can›t know light until we have experienced darkness. We can't *fully* appreciate the stillness and peace of a breath-taking summer sunset without months of frozen winter nights. We can't understand being filled with peace without first being filled with fear. We can't fully have hope without first experiencing a sense of hopelessness. Bitter and sweet.

Perhaps we can't fully say *yes* to showing up with God, until we've felt the intense urgency, to run in the direction of *no*.

Either way, I'm learning I can't truly appreciate a night like tonight, without having walked through the opposite kind of nights, first.

Wouldn't life be easier if slapping a Pinterest-worthy quote on our lives actually worked? *"Keep Calm and Carry On"* anyone? I'm learning the messages the **scriptures** offer are the truth and hope I desperately need during times when everything feels upside down and out of sorts.

They offer what Pinterest never can. While I personally have to fight to believe them and shout *no* to God more times than I'd like to admit, they are the single most important, true, and constant point of guidance in my life.

*"And oh, what joy, and what marvelous light I did behold; yea, **my soul was filled with joy as exceeding as was my pain!** Yea, I say unto you,*

*my son, that there could be nothing so exquisite and so bitter as were my pains. Yea, and again I say unto you, my son,* **that on the other hand, there can be nothing so exquisite and sweet as was my joy,**" (Alma 36:20-21, *The Book of Mormon*).

Alma declared a profound, yet simple truth, one that has brought me hope in my darkest moments. The power of his *yes,* after sin and regret, empowered me in declaring my own *yes* to *all* that God had in store, over not only my life, but my children's as well. If Alma could show up and say *yes,* even after making huge mistakes and wandering very far from God, perhaps I could likewise surrender to God's will. I realized that maybe there really *was* joy on the other side of pain. Light after darkness. Wholeness even after total and utter brokenness. And it was profound.

God consecrates our hard moments and delivers us when we wait on Him in *patience.* When we choose *yes, anyway.*

*But what about the moments in our lives that are hard and uphill of our own doing?*

*Is there still a sweet side to the self-made bitterness in life?*

I once told a lie that twisted my life into something I wasn't sure I could ever come back from. Every day after I spoke those poisonous words, I felt them eating away at my soul. I dreamed about the lie being found out, and about the repercussions of coming clean. I went back and forth daily between what was right and what was very clearly wrong. Stuck in the middle, frozen in fear.

I felt guilt as big as the ocean and regret just as far reaching. I had spun the web of lies, and now I was trapped in my own misery. I cried all the time. I couldn't face God in prayer. I didn't feel worthy of love. There was so much darkness in and around me. I couldn't say *yes* to anything. It was all *no, no, no.*

When I *finally* chose to free myself from that mess of lies, the sense of relief was overwhelming. I could put my life back together. I had been trying, but it was like using Elmer's glue to construct a NASA spaceship.

While that day held its own kind of misery, I felt my soul expand in peace to fill the void where fear and guilt had once lived.

Is it possible then, that God uses even our not-great choices to lead us to *become,* more fully who He knows us to be? Through the power of the Atonement, a relentless *yes* to faith, trust, and truth, fiercely took root in my heart. I can see that even before I spoke a word of truth, before I took a single step toward light, before my heart was turned toward my Savior at all, He was there speaking love over me, and offering strength beyond what I alone possessed.

He will do the same for you, no matter what you've done, how worried, lonely, or lost you may feel. No matter where you've drifted or how much you want to surrender to the darkness. Showing up and choosing *yes* to God, is a sweet joy; one you can only taste after the bitter. The equal and opposite *heavenly joy* that Alma spoke of is *real, powerful*, and *soul-changing*.

## AFFIRMATION:

I will hang onto this truth like my life depends on it. I will choose *yes* to faith, even in the bitter parts of life. There's a sweet side to *yes* with God, and it's everything and more. I am being made ready, *here*. I am in the hands of my Savior, *here*. I am loved, even *here*.

---

He
is
Here

# NARROW BRIDGES

## CHAPTER 13

Out here, the drive to town is a two-lane bendy road littered with tractors hauling apples, onions, and cherries. It's fast speed limits and endless wheat fields. I go through about three times as many tires as the average minivan mom every year.

About halfway to town, there is a small section of road that goes over a ditch as a very narrow bridge. It brings both lanes even closer than they already are, making my heart race a little every time I have to drive over it.

I was on my way to an appointment with the stake president, my ecclesiastical leader at the time, that I'd made as a Hail Mary during the first few days on the path back toward faith. It was raining, and I felt a mixture of embarrassment and desperation--just enough to stop me from canceling the appointment altogether. I was contemplating how my life had gotten so twisty and broken, and how I was going to pick up the pieces, let alone how'd they look once they were together again. *If* they could ever go together again.

I was lost in thought, and that narrow bridge snuck up on me.

I quickly noticed an oncoming semi, and feared that we were going to cross paths on the bridge. I slowed, hoping that would offset our meeting place, but it only seemed to line us up better. Before I knew it, I was gripping the steering wheel with one eye open as we zoomed by each other, nearly touching.

Once safely on the other side, I was suddenly overcome with all the emotions I'd carefully been damming up, behind strong walls of ego and pride. I pulled over as thankful tears gushed out of my eyes.

Recognizing where I was, where I wasn't, and what it would take to alter my current course, was *agonizingly beautiful.*

*"**Come unto the Lord,** the Holy One. Remember that his paths are righteous. Behold, the way for man is **narrow,** but it lieth in a **straight** course before him, and the keeper of the gate is the Holy One of Israel"* (2 *Nephi 9:41, The Book of Mormon*).

***That narrow bridge became a metaphor for my life with God.***

While the world pulls at us in a million ways, trying to deviate us from the narrow and straight path toward God, faith, trust, and Jesus, the truth remains, the way to Him is the less traveled, straight and narrow one. It's a surrendering *yes* to it *all*, no matter what.

That rainy, faith-altering night when I crossed the dreaded narrow bridge changed something within me. The previously overwhelming feelings of guilt, shame, regret, and loss were softened, by a renewed commitment to a life with God, a life with feet firmly planted on narrow bridges, no matter how scary they felt.

Perhaps you aren't on a mission to drastically alter your current path, but are instead weighed down by the narrowness of the paths God has called you to today. Paths you never imagined or asked for.

The tricky thing when opening ourselves up to where we *are*, is that we immediately want to know exactly where we're headed. And in my experience, rarely, if ever, does God show us the end from the beginning.

Winter mornings often engulf our home in a thick frozen fog.

It rolls in from the Columbia River, and everything gets covered in white.

It tends to hang out for days on end, and I start to feel claustrophobic. Driving is both-hands-on-the-steering-wheel-slow, and around every bend I'm praying the other driver is being equally as cautious as me.

And so it goes getting back onto the path toward faith.

I remember all too well choosing *yes* to the first steps of faith: it was like walking out of the warm house, without a coat, into the freezing fog.

Shocking and disorienting.

But I was all in, so I started walking *into* the fog, only able to see a few steps ahead of me at a time. It was fine when I kept my head down and just did my best, but when I started to look around, it was beyond frustrating. I wanted to see the sunshine. I wanted the full scope of this new spiritual landscape. I wanted to see around every curve and bend in the road. I wanted to know *all the time* that I was headed in the right direction, with absolute certainty. I wanted the end right here in this beginning.

It simply wasn't like that.

It was many small steps and *yeses* on a road, that didn't have a party waiting at the end of it. There was no finish line with balloons. Just one step, and another.

*What are **your** steps toward faith?*

I asked that question a lot. And I am coming to believe that they're different for each of us and our unique circumstances. For me at this particular time, they were getting in God's word *every day*. Praying daily, again. And turning off the world for a while, to sort through what I thought and believed, without the constant drip of noise and entertainment and influence.

Have you ever flown over the fog? As the plane climbs, you suddenly emerge into a perfectly blue sky. It is incredible.

That perspective shift changed the way I saw the fog in my spiritual life, and I slowly became comfortable walking into the unknown.

When I walk one foot in front of the other, I have developed trust that He is still there, just as the sun still shines if you get high enough in the sky. It's the absolute truth. **He is there, above it all.**

I think I expected the minute I stepped back onto the narrow path that is faith, there would be clear and sunny skies every day. That wasn't the case, and it was a wakeup call. Once I leaned into the reality that it is *still* worth every effort, *every* moment of fight, and *every* small or big step toward Him, *I got it.*

I understood that we are divine beings living an imperfect human life. We wander and fight to come back. Some days are foggy and we have to focus on each cautious step. Some days are full of sunshine and rainbows. I truly began to accept and lean into *where I was* with arms wide open to *whatever was around the next curve.* Because above all else I began to know without a doubt, that *He was walking beside me.* And choosing *yes* to the daily walk with Him became a way of life.

While I may not know the logistics of your narrow paths, this truth remains. He is there, *right there*, walking that very path alongside you.

The Adversary, on the other hand, loves nothing more than to use the difficult circumstances of our lives, to pull us off the straight and narrow. He will steer us away from faith, convince us that hope is a waste, and that no God would ever make us walk such a dark and hard road. He will make *no* seem logical and reasonable.

He will distract and lead us to poisonous wells. He will encourage anger, frustration, and worry. He will cloud our judgment and dim our internal sense of purpose and light.

Every winter a farmer pastures his herd of sheep near our home. I often pull over on the side of the road to sit and watch them. Their presence always reminds me of the painting of the Savior holding His own beloved sheep tenderly in His arms.

*"Suppose one of you has a hundred sheep and loses one of them. Doesn't he leave the ninety-nine in the open country and go after the lost sheep until he finds it? And when he finds it, he joyfully puts it on his shoulders and goes home. Calling his friends and neighbors together and says, 'Rejoice with me;*

***I have found my lost sheep,'"*** *(Luke 15:4-7, New International Version).*

*Where are you right now?*

*What narrow bridges are you being called to walk over?*

*What's stopping you on the other side?*

I will never deny that Christ leaves the ninety-nine to find the one. Even when that one is you or me. Even when the one is reckless, wandering, and doubting. There is no distance or fog or darkness that He won't go to find you. He knows **you**--your weaknesses, your fears, your whole self. The good, the bad, and all of it in-between.

We are all a mixed bag. *But He isn't.*

He is the life, light, and the way. Unchanging and unwavering.

I'm learning a truly committed life over narrow bridges is often foggy, and allows nothing but one step at a time. Sometimes, it's just glimmers of hope and peace and love in unfair circumstances. It's hope in tomorrows. It's grace when we wander, and love when we mess it all up. It's Hail Marys that alter your entire life, and crack open the darkness with unexplainable light. It's second chances and Him, right HERE.

*Here* in the middle of the darkest night.

*Here* in your want, your doubt, and your fear.

*Here* in your deep regret, in the losing fight, in the fiercest storm.

*Here* in the quiet waiting.

*Here* in every season, on every straight and narrow path.

## AFFIRMATION:

I will hang on, no matter what. I will recommit every day if necessary, to stay strong on each straight, narrow, and often less traveled road toward Him.

**He will be there with me, even right *here*.**

_____

_____

_____

_____

_____

_____

_____

_____

_____

_____

_____

_____

_____

_____

_____

_____

_____

_____

_____

_____

Courtney Casper ...

♡ ◻ ▽

# DARKNESS

## CHAPTER 14

It's October now and the sun is taking longer and longer to rise. Our two school-aged girls keep sleeping in late, so this morning I had Alexa play *"Here Comes the Sun"* to get them going. I heard them groan from all the way in the kitchen downstairs. I feel their tired pains on these early mornings.

That half hour when I'm the only one awake is strange in the dark. In the summer with the sun shining at 5am, that time feels invigorating. But the fall and winter months are different. They feel hushed and sacred. And admittedly, a bit sleepy.

Lynley may dread the dark mornings getting up for school, but I'm learning something through them. I'm leaning into their darkness, trying to welcome it, because in those dark minutes I'm forced to open my eyes and settle in, while I wait for dawn.

*"The people which sat in darkness saw great light,"* (Matthew 4:16, King James Version).

I'll never forget the first time I came out here to Basin City, 25 miles from town. Standing in the cold fall air, looking up at the black sky, I had never seen so many stars. And not just stars, but the entire Milky Way was showing off, and I was in *awe*.

In the words of Florence and the Machine, *"It's always darkest before the dawn."*

That hour before dawn breaks is special. There's nothing to do but be there and *wait in the dark*.

I used to fight darkness and wonder what was wrong with me when I felt *"in"* it. I'd walk around feeling shame and anger, trying to outrun, outsmart, and outshine the darkness. I tried to *be* the sun. Create it for myself through productivity and hustle. Spoiler: it never worked.

I'm learning that darkness isn't a scarlet letter; **it's sacred ground**. It's where God does some of His best work in us. It's where our *yeses* are tested and turned into lasting roots of faith and trust.

My quiet, dark mornings demand stillness. They embrace smallness. They open the door to true presence.

I'm learning about presence over productivity. When we are in the dark, we have to stop running so dang fast. Like my kids playing hide and go seek tag in the dark. I warn them over and over to slow down and stop running, to avoid serious head wounds on every corner of every wall. When we're walking through dark seasons of our lives, it's tempting to speed up, go into overdrive, and out produce the darkness.

But I'm learning that true presence with God, with the people around us, and with ourselves trumps the importance of productivity at every turn. *Especially* in the dark as we wait for dawn.

Racing into productive mode when we're wrestling with darkness is just as dangerous for our heart and soul as playing hide and go seek tag in the dark. We risk the very real possibility of wounding our faith and trust in our Father who *is* there, even in our wrestle toward light.

When we truly learn the art of presence over productivity, the dark isn't something to fear at all. The seasons of darkness begin to remake our stories, our hearts, and our wild *yes* to God, in *all* that he calls us to become.

Going dark from the hustle and noise of the world opens my eyes to this one and only life I'm living, and the light all around me.

A social media fast or waking before dawn isn't so bad because we choose it. We are at the helm of those *yeses*, and so trusting that light will come is not so hard to believe.

*But what about the times when the darkness slowly creeps into our lives, casting a shadow where light once was?* Having to wait through times when the heavens seem silent and the path ahead is unknown is much more difficult. However, being forced to sit in the darkness when you are desperate for enlightenment, is some of the *most* important soul work you will ever do.

**And it is as hard, as it is profound.**

Experiencing darkness, while frustrating as it may be, is where we find out what is worth waiting for, trusting in, and hoping for.

Divine Darkness, what I'm calling it, is something I'm learning to welcome instead of resist. It's where I get small and quiet and open myself up to listen and feel. It's where I learn and push roots deep into the cold earth, waiting for seasons of growth to eventually come.

When I reflect on the times in my life that I was most on fire in my faith, they are always on the other side of a season spent waiting with God, in the dark.

Before deeply studying The Book of Mormon, I was almost certain it was something I never wanted to read again. A strong compelling force led me to it, and I followed hesitantly. It had been decades of not engaging in The Book of Mormon, but after the first chapter, I felt a fire burning in my soul.

I cried finishing that book a few months later. I had never felt that kind of faith on fire. I had never felt such intense truth wash over me: that book *is* the Word of God.

I share that fire with my children again and again. I have stood at the pulpit of my tiny church family and bore witness more times in the last few years, than in my whole life put together. I shout it from the internet rooftops, despite those who disagree and politely leave shortly after. I am all-in to speak truth as long as *one* person hears it. I will go and do, in the name of this newfound fire and *yes* to God.

*"What I tell you in darkness, that speak ye in light: and what ye hear in the ear, that preach ye upon the housetops,"* (Matthew 10:27, *King James Version*).

I am convinced that those years waiting to know if The Book of Mormon was true, created an equal and opposite space for a life changing shift, when God decided it was time. He enlightened my whole soul right when I was at an important crossroads in my life. I **waited** *and He broke the dawn.*

It's *in* the dark that we can see the hand of God most clearly.

Being in the dark is when we *truly* appreciate the light.

## AFFIRMATION:

I choose *yes* to trusting, even in the dark; That eventually the sun *will* rise again.

And when it does, He will work wonders in and through my life in a million little ways that *set my soul on fire.*

_____

_____

_____

_____

_____

_____

_____

_____

_____

_____

_____

_____

_____

Find a
COURAGEOUS
yes to it
all.

Courtney Casper ...

♡ ◯ ⊲

# TIME 𝄢 TIME

## CHAPTER 15

It's become a theme in my life, as you well know by now, this thing between faith and me. We ebb and we flow. We sink a little and then walk on water. Instead of panicking each time I feel the waves crashing around my knees, I just keep holding on knowing this season will pass, and through it, faith will be mine once again.

"The Book of Mormon Project," was a project to reformat the Book of Mormon into something with room to journal, spiral bound, and with artwork from a handful of other artists with verses of scripture that changed their lives. It was a rescue rope thrown to me during a season of spiritual sinking. In order to make this project happen, first I had to pivot my entire business and online platform, from hand lettering into something much more personal and vulnerable. To something I was still very much learning myself.

After it came to me I started almost immediately, putting every other artistic effort on hold. My Instagram page was not yet covered in faith-based messages--and to make this big jump felt scary. But I knew deep in my heart where this particular project was coming from, and so I said *yes* and pushed forward in faith.

After figuring out how to create a wide margin Book of Mormon and enlisting the twenty or so other artists of faith to share their talents through this inspired project, it was created and released into the world.

*God is good. That project is proof.*

There have since been many other divinely inspired projects, none of which I felt qualified to create. *This book is at the top of that list.* They were born through brave *yeses* to the whisperings of the Spirit, and my willing hands and heart. Sleepless nights seem to follow me through each endeavor, as I wonder if I am doing and saying the right things. Even small *yeses,* like sharing personal spiritual thoughts online, don't go without some wrestling. This book is pushing me beyond where I've gone before, and each step feels scary.

When reading in 1 Nephi 17 (The Book of Mormon), I am so inspired by Nephi's conversion to a God who will lead and direct His people, working miracles even, on their behalf. You might know these chapters well. We read about the hardships Nephi and his family faced over the course of eight years in the wilderness. We also hear about Nephi's brothers' personal struggles to continue on in such circumstances. They were done. And if I'm honest, with good reason.

But Nephi doesn't accept this way of thinking. Not for one second does he indulge in a negative attitude or doubt. He responds to his brothers' outcries of anger and even murderous rebellion with conviction second to none: "*If the Lord has such great power to work miracles of all kinds, impossible and unseen with the children of God, why would I doubt that he can and will do the same for me?"* (1 Nephi 17:51, *The Book of Mormon, paraphrased*).

Nephi, after eight years of faithfully choosing *yes* to his own walk with God, years of following and being led, was then asked to build a boat.

A BOAT!

He tells us humbly that he has no clue how to accomplish such a crazy thing. He doesn't know what tools he needs, where to get them, or even where this boat will be taking his family, assuming that it floats.

A lot of solid and logical reasons to politely say, *no thanks.*

But it seemed nothing could discourage his faith and trust that had led them up to that point.

After convincing his doubting brothers that he would, in fact, follow through on this errand, we read in the first verse of 1 Nephi 18 (The Book of Mormon), three words that shake me to my core.

Nephi does *not* say that while on the Lord's abstract and difficult errand of building a ship he was given every step of the plan, that the tools appeared, their purpose self-explanatory, or that every morning he woke up with a bulleted to-do list or master instructional manual.

Which I'm pretty sure is what I would require to choose *yes* in this call to action.

But, no. Not Nephi.

He says that as they worshipped the Lord, worked hard, and trusted, God showed him *"from time to time,"* what he should do to build this ship.

Perhaps, the reason those words jump off the page for me is because as I sit at my kitchen table now, keeping me company is a pile of unanswered questions about the next few months. Desires from the depths of my heart, with only silent heavens to plead to.

When those lulls in communication come, I find myself getting more frustrated with each passing day. *Where is God? Why isn't He answering me now? He's guided and directed me so clearly in the past, why all this silence now?*

After frustration comes the doubt. *Am I on the right path at all? Was that initial inspiration wrong? Was it all just in my own head?*

By now we know that I am no Nephi, but I am confident that God loves me just the same. If while on God's seemingly impossible errand of ship building, Nephi was given direction from **time to time,** *why am I expecting something different? Why am I anticipating a vision of the future every night? A clear path every morning?*

I'm learning faith is walking on the paths that God calls us to, *without* the constant flow of praise, success, or even guidance for every step. It's *continually moving*, even when you're not sure where you're going. It's surrendering to His will, even when the way forward is unclear and strewn with setbacks, unknowns, or heartaches as deep as the sea.

Choosing *yes* to it *all*, requires faith in a million small ways. But I'm learning when silence takes the place of guidance, your *yes* becomes a *life-altering* **yes.**

*Are the heavens empty if no one's talking from them this minute?*

*Can you hold on during the in-between seasons that Nephi describes as God's "time to time" inspiration?*

I'm coming to deeply believe, holding onto faith during the seasons of life that are on fire with heavenly inspiration and guidance is one thing. But to truly become converted and changed into who God designed us to be, we *must* find a courageous *yes* to the roads that are filled with echoing silence too.

## AFFIRMATION:

**Yes.** *Yes*, I will hold on. I will continue walking through all seasons-- fog, doubt, fear, and anxiety. I will hold on and trust in the God who delivers His people with miracles seen and unseen. Because I am His, through it *all.*

_____

_____

_____

_____

_____

_____

_____

_____

_____

He
will
hear
your
cries

♡ ⊙ ⎘

# CHAPTER 16

Our kids wear boots on a regular basis. I have hardwood floors, mainly because those muddy boots make their way across the kitchen on the daily, along with muddy paw prints from Max, our black Goldendoodle. Tyler actually makes his fair share of muddy entrances too, now that I think of it.

The temperature hit 60 today. It was a cloudy 60, but after a long, cold winter it might as well have been 90, and the girls thought it was summer. I let them run out the door like wild animals after we got home from our town errands.

I left them to their imaginary world of moms, fairies, and ponies and went to unload the groceries from our car.

In the thick of unpacking Costco boxes and rearranging pantry and fridge shelves I heard a faint *"Mom! Mom!"* coming from the closed back door. My littlest, two and a half at the time, couldn't open the door yet, so I kept an ear out for her call when she needed me.

As I opened the door, I was met by two muddy hands covering her eyes and just two words, *"Hands dirty."* She had found her favorite thing: **mud.**

She loves the mud but doesn't love her fingers caked in it. Which causes lots of problems in a two-year-old's world.

Knowing she was going to go right back to the mud, but not wanting the toddler melt down I knew all too well, I grabbed a cloth and wiped her hands with a *"Ta-da!"* to really sell the idea that her hands were clean, even though they weren't *clean*, clean. Just clean enough.

This happened a few more times.

When she was ready for popcorn, I carried her into the house and to my white farmhouse kitchen sink. She knew the drill. Hands outstretched towards the running water, I took those little dimpled hands and began to wash them clean.

Although the mud was dried in layers, the warm water quickly washed them all away, leaving behind fresh fingers again.

*And then, tears welled up in my eyes.*

With the mud still swirling around my kitchen sink, she looked up at me with her crazy head of curls and big blue eyes and said in a very serious voice, *"All clean, mom."*

Just like that.

**All clean.**

I couldn't help but feel God in that moment.

Life has a way of mudding us up. Our hearts. Our minds. Our lives. Sometimes we knowingly walk over to the puddle and sink our hands deep into the cold, wet mud. Maybe even again and again. Sometimes the mud comes from others. Just as Callie came in upset because of her sisters' aimless flinging hands, that had resulted in mud on her cheeks and nose. The choices of others, actions of others, or circumstances involving others can weigh on us, and alter our own sense of well-being.

Regardless of *how* the mud got there, I bet we can all agree that each of us encounters mud, maybe even daily.

However, just like washing Elaine's tiny, muddy hands under the running water, our Savior does the same for us. He is the running water. His Spirit the other set of hands. Together they wash us clean from the mud of our lives.

I'm learning that while I tend to overthink *how* it all works, *why* it all works, and *if* it will work for *me*, we simply need to turn on the water and outstretch our hands. His purifying love is there to wash away our heartaches, loneliness, sin, and sorrow. Our frustrations and self-doubt. Every pain and tear shed. Being determined to carry around those burdens is like living with mud spattered on our cheeks or between our fingers. It's uncomfortable, and altogether unnecessary. Not to mention, it drips on those around us. It gets on everything we touch. It smudges our relationships, marriages, and our life's work.

It's possible to *sort of* wash it away. Just like I did with the dry towel the first, second, and third time my girl wanted to be cleaned up. The halfhearted dusting off *kind of* worked. It pacified her for a few more minutes. But then she was right back to the mud. As if she knew that a little more wouldn't hurt what was still left behind. We can, likewise, teeter on the edge of choosing *yes* to trusting the Savior's healing powers.

*Mostly* using the Savior's Atonement may pacify us for a second. It might make us feel a *little* better. But going back to the mud will be less shocking than the first time. The cold won't be as cold. The dirt not as uncomfortable. After all, we're already sort of muddy, *what's a little more?*

I love the story in the New Testament found in Luke 17. The chapter starts with Jesus telling his apostles *"If ye had faith as a grain of mustard seed, ye might say unto this sycamore tree, be thou plucked up by the root, and be thou planted in the sea; and it should obey you,"* (Luke 17:6, King James Version).

*Have you ever seen those two things? A mustard seed and a sycamore tree?*

I recently bought a necklace with a tiny mustard seed encapsulated by a glass pendant. It's small and delicate, a constant reminder that even when my faith is equally as small and fragile, the power granted through Jesus is *more* than enough. My courageous declaration of trust and faith matters, even if it's tiny.

Comparatively, the sycamore tree is so large it reaches far and wide into the sky. We used to live under a sycamore. The roots crawled across most of the large yard, its leaves are bigger than my face. We'd rake piles and piles of leaves each year, and I have many treasured photos of two tiny girls at sunset on the beloved tire swing, that hung from its large and sturdy branches.

Coming back to a life lived with faith and trust, this analogy has kept me company many long days and nights. I wondered if *I* could possibly continue on. If *I* could possibly be made whole. If *I* could ever really believe again. **A mustard seed.** I would look at myself in the mirror with the tiny pendant around my neck and assure myself, that, **yes**, I could have a little amount of faith today. Surely I could manage even just that.

I eventually learned that our faith need not be as big as a sycamore tree to say *yes* to *all* God calls us to. It only takes a small amount of faith to outstretch our hands to the cleansing water of Christ's Atonement and love. *It really does.* I know, because I've been there: painfully aware of the mud on my hands but scared to death to reach out to Him.

*Maybe he'll turn me away. Maybe I'm not worth it. Maybe it doesn't matter. Maybe I don't matter. Maybe I'm too far gone.*

But then I think of Elaine. She was never embarrassed or afraid to come to me when she needed to be cleaned up. She fully trusted and relied on me, and didn't hesitate to reach her hands out over and over again. Confident in my ability to rinse the mud away, she never once stood outside the door contemplating if she was worthy enough to call my name. She simply called out, and I was there.

*"For the natural man is an enemy to God, and has been from the fall of Adam, and will be, forever and ever, **unless** he yields to the enticings of the Holy Spirit, and putteth off the natural man and becometh as a child, submissive, meek, humble, patient, full of love, willing to submit to all things which the Lord seeth fit to inflict upon him, even as a child doth submit to his father,"* (Mosiah 3:19, The Book of Mormon).

I think it's natural and human that we want to figure life out on our own. Maybe at eight years old we would find our own way to wash our hands. Maybe by 16, we would try to sneak in the house and wash our hands ourselves, not wanting to cause a scene. By our late twenties and into our thirties, we're pretending there's no mud at all, confident in our own ability to hide and cover up what's underneath. And on and on and on.

But I'm learning that I cannot bear the weight of this world alone, I cannot hide the mud. Instead I repeat in my mind over and over *"He is my Father... my Father."* I picture myself as His child, willing myself to be trusting and confident in His love and unwavering care. I will myself to rely on whatever sized faith I have, to show up, call out, and act in obedience. I will myself to choose *yes*.

*Yes*, to trust in His timeline and submission to His plans and purposes. *Yes*, to retraining my impatient and fearful heart to be patient and open instead. *Yes*, to releasing my pride and self-doubt to become more like Elaine, confident and humble. *Yes*, to standing outside the back door when I need help cleaning the mud and saying, *"Jesus, Jesus,"* trusting that He *will* be there to open it.

As the chapter in Luke (17:19-21) continues, we learn of ten lepers "standing afar off," from Jesus. They call to him and stretch forth their hands. They find faith the size of a mustard seed, even in all their pain, worry, and doubts.

I've tried to put myself in their shoes. They were dealing with a physical condition so painful and alienating, that it was quite literally, taking over their entire lives. Maybe their pain didn't end on the surface, maybe they suffered wounds just as deep and painful on an emotional and spiritual level as well. Maybe those deep wounds aren't as obvious but just as gut wrenching.

*Who of us hasn't experienced such suffering in one way or another? Who of us hasn't felt the burning desperation for deliverance?* We learn from these lepers that it doesn't matter how far away we're standing from Jesus. When we raise our voices to Him, He *will* hear our cries.

Read that again: **He *will* hear *your* cries.**

And you know what? He doesn't tell them to do anything grand or flashy. He asks them to choose *yes* in obedience, which all ten do. In return they are all healed from their physical affliction. *Healed,* just like that.

After all was said and done, only one of the ten lepers turned back to glorify God.

Just one.

Of course, Jesus doesn't smite down the other nine. Instead He takes a moment for the grateful one and declares that his *faith had made him whole.* Not just physically healed, but *whole.* There's a difference here, and I wonder what we are to learn from this account.

Maybe even kind of engaging the Atonement brings miracles into our lives. Maybe even faith just the size of a mustard seed *is* enough for healing. But maybe Jesus is hinting to us that when we truly come unto Him, *all* in, through *all* seasons, *always,* there is more for us.

Wholeness. Wholeness in secret places of our aching heart and soul. In things unspoken, and unknown by the world. These splotches of mud that we tuck away and hide are made whole through our childlike submission and patience and gratitude toward our Savior.

Maybe Christ is reaching our reaching, desiring us to more fully use the gift that has already been bought and paid for, His Atonement.

*Have you ever experienced that kind of healing? That kind of purification? That kind of love? A relief from burden, pain, and suffering?*

There are many times that my Savior has cleansed me. Reached my fragile reaching. Cleansed my dirty hands. Stitched together my broken heart. Each time with careful love and empathy, taking time to gently cleanse each part of me. Spiritually. Emotionally. Mentally. And physically.

*Yes, yes, yes.*

Through our personal sacrifices to bravely choose *yes* to Jesus, offering ourselves totally, we too will witness miracles seen and unseen. We too can have access to a power that changes us--mind, body, and spirit. As we are laser-focused on the goodness of God and the power of the Atonement, our gratitude gifts us wholeness that *lasts.*

No more mud on hands. No more splatters on cheeks. No more heavy burdens and disrupted peace. Not a trace.

As the warm water ran over Elaine's tiny and trusting hands, God whispered to my soul, *"I am here. To love. To cleanse. To purify. YOU."*

## AFFIRMATION:

*I* am a child of God. Jesus Christ is *my* Savior. There is healing and wholeness as I bravely outstretch my hands and heart to Him. I will reach and He will reach out to me in return. I am worthy of His love. I have the power to access the Atonement, and begin a new life in Christ.

_____

_____

_____

_____

_____

_____

_____

_____

_____

_____

_____

_____

_____

_____

_____

_____

_____

_____

face &
reflect
LiGHT.

Courtney Casper  ...

♡ ▢ ∇

# ReBELLioN

## CHAPTER 17

Have you ever seen a group of cows together? It's the strangest thing. They huddle together, and then out of the blue one will get a little pep in her step and start running. She suddenly decides to run to nowhere in particular, and they all think they had better follow.

The whole herd of cows running for no reason to nowhere all happens because one cow picks up their pace.

So often I hear from the women who connect with me online, a resounding *sigh*. Because we're all so busy, so tired, so burned out, and so full outside noise. Our intentions slip between our fingers. We want to do and be all the good things, but somehow end up a slave to our endless hustle.

Just because we see someone else running does not mean we have to chase after them. The huddle of cows don't mean any harm in their following, but what they choose to chase *does* matter. They end up in different pastures, whether that decision was conscious or not.

*Can you relate? Do you ever find yourself running, just for the sake of running? Chasing and following things or people or ideas that you never consciously chose? Marching and hustling in exchange for your soul space and rest?*

Over the last few years I've committed to starting a rebellion of sorts. I want to rebel against the ties I feel the world is desperately trying to confine me by. It constantly attempts to suffocate my spiritual fire with busyness, stunt my personal growth with crippling expectations, and steal my joy with comparison and self-doubt. Feeding me reasons as to why faith and hope and trust are the things logical people say *"no thank you"* to.

I was sitting on the couch with Elaine, a few days ago. We've been engulfed in fog the last week, but this particular morning the sun was finally coming through the mist, pouring into our large family room windows. We were alone in the house and I had made great efforts to ignore my to-do list, and just sit with my curly haired 4-year-old for a few minutes of quiet, and sunshine.

Elaine is very introspective and often stares into my eyes longer than is humanly comfortable. This morning she got close, I mean *really* close, and said *"Mom, I can see the sun in your eyes when you look at the windows."*

As I looked into hers, I could see *my* reflection in *her* big blue eyes. She saw light in me as I turned toward light.

I'm learning that where I'm turned and what I'm facing reflects in every aspect of my life. In my motherhood, work, sisterhood, and in my marriage. All of it. In all the things.

If we're facing *light*, light is reflected outward. When we're facing comparison, and envy and lack, its reflected in our thoughts, feelings, and emotions. Those things spill out and into how we act, react, and live.

I often find myself focused on what *I* have to offer the Lord. My busyness, my service, my fully checked off to-do list. When my focus is there, however, I find myself often looking around at what everyone else is offering. Sometimes I even find myself chasing whomever seems to be running the fastest, offering the most, or looks to be the most productive.

In Colossians 3:17 we learn something about what God thinks of our to-do lists: *"And whatsoever ye do in word or deed, do all in the name of the Lord Jesus, giving thanks to God and the Father by him."*

I'm learning the hard way, that instead of focusing my time, energy, and soul space on what *I* have to offer the Lord, I'd be wiser to consider what the Lord is offering *me*.

God never asked any of us to sacrifice our soul for any*thing* or any*one* besides Him. He never asked us to be the great I Am. We are *not* I Am. *He is.*

*Are we consciously choosing to live our lives in His name, giving thanks for what He offers, instead of making ourselves feel better about our unmet intentions by glorifying what we can produce and offer the world?*

In the united *sigh* and *"I'm just too busy"* or *"I don't have time,"* I want to shake you awake to the lie that the Adversary is packaging up real pretty and shoving into your arms. He wants you under the very convincing and convenient impression that your hands are tied.

That you are bound by invisible chains that demand you spend your time in any such way. That you should run after the people you see running. He wants you to truly believe that you are a slave to screens and media and lies, about needing perfect children in coordinating outfits in a home with freshly mopped floors. He wants you to believe that you are on your own, doomed to live a life on a hamster wheel, where you never measure up, are always tired, less than, and alone in it all.

**Lies. Lies. Lies.**

My closet is almost never clean. I try, but after a few days the shoes pile up and the discarded outfits join the party on the floor. But it is my little refuge, nonetheless.

To someone passing by, it may seem like a windowless hodge-podge of gray and striped t-shirts, jeans, and tennis shoes, but to me, it's *my* place. I pray there. I sit there and reflect, listen, and give space for my soul to inhale and exhale.

At any point in your day, you have the absolute power to declare it restful or reflective. You are not bound by any chain, list, or required productivity—you get to decide when to run and when to stop.

Of course, there are some things that may seem mandatory, but are they really? *Are they really?*

I can tell you that now, there *are* a few things in my days that are mandatory: prayer, scripture study, and a quieted soul. Some days the quiet and prayer are mixed together in meditation on the back porch. When the anxiety is tight in my chest those mandatory things are done under my weighted blanket. Sometimes they're done in the grocery pickup line through my headphones. Rain or shine, day or night, formal or informal, they make all the difference in my days. And they make: **The Mandatory List.**

If those things are an absolute must for me, then other things do not get to take their place. They do not get to steal my focus or energy away from them. I choose *yes* to God in these ways, even if it means *no* to something else.

My floors may not get mopped. I may not know what's happening on Facebook. I may not get a shower, and I might not answer those emails. But spending time and energy with God through intentional prayer and scripture study, is worth it to me, a thousand times over.

**Your spiritual health matters more than being "productive."** More than serving others even. More than clean floors or burning calories. *More than anything.*

**You are not powerless.** In fact, God is known for giving His faithful followers the power to overcome each stumbling block that stands in their way.

The world today sometimes feels like our own personal Goliath.

Goliath screamed at the Israelites for 40 days, demanding someone to come and challenge him. *Forty days.* The world is just as relentless on you and me. Social media and our amazingly useful, yet addicting, phones will draw us in *relentlessly.* Our small doubts will chip away at our faith *relentlessly.* The demands on our time will *never* ease up. There will always be someone who seems to be doing life better and faster.

Goliaths. Giants yelling in our faces, demanding something from us.

After many people called David crazy for even considering going up against Goliath, he boldly declared his faith and trust in the Lord's deliverance, found his five stones, and went up against the giant. He said *yes* anyway.

Goliath mocked David, called him worthless, and didn't even flinch at the young boy's advances toward him.

*"Then said David to the Philistine, Thou comest to me with a sword, and with a spear, and with a shield: but I come to thee in the name of the Lord of hosts, the God of the armies of Israel, whom thou hast defied,"* (Samuel 17:45, King James Version).

You know the rest; David and God defeat the enemy by unreasonable means. Logic is clear, one small stone doesn't kill a Goliath. But God works in mysterious ways, and they go beyond the sense of logic in our lives just the same.

We are not cows. We are not followers of the world; we don't *have* to heed the lies of the Adversary. We get to declare *yes* to God instead, and walk a path of trust, faith, prayer, and study. We get to live a life of connectedness to our Heavenly Parents. We get to choose a path of rest with a heart turned to Jesus. We get to stand still and know in whom we trust. We can rely on the unreasonable-ness of our Father to work miracles in our lives. We get to designate closets a refuge, carpools our precious scripture study time, and morning walks for quiet reflection. We get to face light if we choose, reflecting God's love in every part of our lives. We get to run when we feel called to run, letting others do the same without the compulsion to keep up or chase after them.

We were created children of God in His image.

He never spoke hustle into our souls.

He simply said, *"Be still and know."*

## AFFIRMATION:

I will contemplate what is truly mandatory in my days, making my own **Mandatory List.** I will consciously choose to create sacred time and space for reflection, prayer, and study. I will not heed the sneaky lies of the Adversary. I am not powerless to anything or anyone. I can rely on God's strength in my weakness. I am His child. I am strong. I am loved.

_____

_____

_____

_____

_____

_____

_____

_____

_____

_____

_____

_____

what is essential today?

♡ ❏ ⊽

# *Less*

## CHAPTER 18

Facebook recently thought I'd really enjoy an article titled, "*Ten Ways to Fake Rested.*" The tips included fancy eye creams and hydration serums to hide the dark circles under tired eyes, caffeine to mask the exhaustion, and encouragement to move yet even *faster,* to hide the lack of capacity and energy.

Thanks for nothing, Facebook.

Coming back to faith, I knew a few things needed to change in my day to day, changes that would require great effort and purposeful choices. Sacrifices even. The first of which was honestly taking inventory of where I spent my time.

We *all* have the same 24 hours a day, seven days a week. We *all* have hard days and responsibilities that pile up. Some seasons of our lives are overwhelming just to get from hour to hour. Health, finances, relationships, and a slew of other struggles can bog us down and begin to steal more time and energy than we'd like. I began to see clearly that if I was *really* going to remake my life from the inside out, if I was *really* going to pivot and change my current *soul* circumstance, I was going to have to take an *honest* look at my life and rearrange some of it.

If you'd asked me even a year ago to describe myself, I would have most definitely said something about how "highly capable" I was.

In my not-so-fun-experience, holding onto the idea that I am "highly capable," does not serve me well. My version of "highly capable" looks a lot like running myself ragged at whatever cost necessary. And when I'm sprinting through life things slip through the cracks. Lots of "stuff" might get accomplished, but I am 100% more likely to lose it on my kids and family. I "forget" to say my prayers. I'm "too tired" to read my scriptures. And, with the wind whipping through my hair, my heart cannot be heard over the deafening speed of all my capable-ness.

There is serious power in the self-discipline of intentionally deciding the size and speed of our lives. Fully letting go of this crazy and toxic idea that our highly capable-ness creates our worth, allows our eyes to refocus on where our worth truly comes from.

After a particularly insane week I vowed that Monday, I would rest. I would sleep and eat real food and slow down. I would do it, no matter what. When Monday came, I had the tempting realization that my daily mile needed walked, the laundry needed folded, the emails had piled up overnight, and the dishes weren't done. I was painfully aware of so many things that seemed to reach out, and literally, demand a piece of me.

After getting the older two off to school, instead of succumbing to the ever-looming draw of busyness that called my name, I made a conscious decision to get back into bed with my scriptures, instead.

I pulled Elaine into bed with me and together we snuggled. She watched Tinker Bell and I wrote and read. When I declared us rested, I could see the renewal in even her eyes. She needed that time as much as I did. Before tucking her in that night, I asked what the best part of her day was. Without hesitation she responded, *"Our bed snuggling party! I want more of that."*

**The impact of less is real.** And it reaches way beyond ourselves.

It's tempting to look at faith and say: **be grown.**

It's tempting to expect it to be there, flourishing, always.

But I'm learning over and over again, that's not reality. The reality is: what I water, grows. And that growth happens slowly, over time, in natural seasons.

I have a small section of dirt next to my house that I've claimed as my herb garden. It includes two basil plants, one rosemary, and a yellow pepper. For being a faux farm girl, I may have missed the *"What's an herb,"* informational workshop.

At any rate, it's *my* tiny piece of dirt. I planted the starts and I have to remember to kick on the water every other day, so that amazing fresh basil doesn't dry up.

Watering faith isn't so different.

It requires physical and mental sacrifice and action. And for me, the first daily step is carving out space, energy, and quiet in my life, that is not very spacious or quiet. Especially in the midst of a full-blown summer vacation with four kids, a dog, a husband, a job, church responsibilities, friend duties, neighbor duties, things like laundry, and heaven forbid I hop in the shower! Or maybe you have a job, or two! A new puppy. Chronic illness. Mental struggles. If creating space for our souls to connect with God was easy, we'd all be doing it 6 hours a day. But, that's simply not reality.

You know what is easy to water?

A social media addiction. A Netflix season 12 situation. A really good novel. A half marathon training program. These things pay off in ways that, I don't know, are measurable and recognizable. You can gold star a workout. You can gain another follower. You can discuss the latest scandal. You can binge another season.

Make no mistake, we *are* watering stuff every day.

We're pouring into our people. Into our health. Into our homes and jobs and actual fiddle leaf house plants. (I haven't managed to kill mine yet. Fingers crossed for her.)

Here's the thing: if we're struggling in our faith and not sure why that is, maybe it's time to take an honest look, if we're watering it? Consistently? Is it on the to-do list, if not at the very tippy-top of it? Is it the first thing on our mind, and the last thing before bed? Is it an absolutely must do, at-all-costs type of priority? What we starve *will* stop growing, and the things we water, *will* **grow.**

Ugh.

I know. I know it all too well.

I'm going to be brutally honest and vulnerable with you here, if I have the time to research jean jackets on sale (my personal weakness) and meal plans, and know what an acquaintance had for breakfast during her beach vacation, **I have the time to study my scriptures.** If I have time to watch a 30-minute episode of "The Office" while eating lunch (another personal favorite; now you *really* know all my dirty laundry), **I have the time to study my scriptures.** If I have the time to scroll through Instagram, which I do multiple times a day, (feel free to insert Facebook, the latest news cycle, or YouTube here) **I have the time to pray.**

Pulling back my social media use, I found so much more with so much *less*. Less noise. Less distraction. Less time wasted focused on a screen. There was *more* thinking, *more* laughing, *more* seeing and hearing. I watched my kids while they played, I wrote more than ever. There was time and space for things that I never seemed to have time for in my regular life. It was eye opening and heart softening to realize, within my allotted 24 hours a day, I had *plenty* of everything I needed to live the intentional life I longed for, free from eternal exhaustion and distraction.

I had said *yes* to one thing, and with it said *no* to others. Saying *yes* to less, is becoming a way to truly make a valuable impact that matters in my life. Saying *no* to things like rushing and distraction is coincidentally, creating more *yeses* that count.

Each morning in prayer I ask God, "*What is essential of me today?*" I don't just ask, "*What is important?*" because to me, it tends to *all* be important. I'm just one of those people. I care *too* much about *too* much. I really like to hang onto my capable-ness. But I'm changing the question and it is changing the answers I receive.

*What is **essential** for **me**, today?*

The narrative that somehow my life had to be a certain size and be lived at a certain pace was a lie. If we continue to do the same things we are doing, we will get the same results we've been getting.

We get to choose our *yeses.*

Our committed *yes* in unwavering faith, to *all* that God calls us to, is not something that is one-and-done. We can't read scriptures for an hour on Monday and expect to fight the good fight for the next six days. Our faith is not a sprint; it's a slow and steady *daily* walk. It's small bites and, maybe, shrinking the size of our checklist and reducing the speed at which we accomplish those things, to make time for *more. More* reflection, *more* pondering, *more* studying, and *more* stillness.

Being highly capable is overrated in my book. In my book, being capable enough is the sweet spot. And at the end of the day, none of it gets to be tied to our worth.

The price to pay in ignoring the small whisper toward less is steep. We'll find it easier and easier to turn our hearts with a stubborn *"no"* to faith and trust. Because there will never magically be time to fully nurture that faith, without the self-discipline to make it a top priority.

*Doing faith in spurts is just not enough.*

If we're tired and burned out, circumstances have the ability to steer us off course and steal our peace and hope. If we're maxed out, focused on all the things that don't truly matter, it's all too easy to believe the sneaky lies of the Adversary.

And he's going all out. He will move heaven and earth to convince us that success and busyness are everything. He will bombard us with traps of comparison and crippling self-doubt. He will encourage us to run faster than we have strength, robbing us of so, *so* much.

Your soul was never meant to be a sacrifice for any amount of checked off boxes. Your faith was never intended to be an offering on the altar of busyness. Your time was not given to be squandered on things that just don't matter in the end.

God doesn't require you to check off a list of worship each day. He doesn't ask for a specific word count in prayer. He simply calls your name and says, *"Come unto me."*

I used to think that I should only come unto Him once everything else was done, because, you know, I'm highly capable and all. Now I'm seeing that when I come in all my undoneness, He resets and refocuses everything in a way that I can't do on my own. When I am deeply connected to Him, my days don't blur into one long 24 hours, they are shaped and *intentionally* lived.

*"It's not always that we need to do more but rather that we need to focus on less,"* (Nathan W. Morris).

_____

_____

_____

_____

_____

_____

Courtney Casper

♡ ⎘ ⩔

# ÇABBATH

## CHAPTER 19

A few years ago, I had a burning desire to understand why I observed the Sabbath. I had been raised to observe the Sabbath most of my life in a traditional Latter-day Saint home. We didn't shop on Sundays, go out to eat, and we attended church. Pretty typical.

Those traditions stayed with me through college and into adulthood, but in the last few years, I desired to figure out *why in the world* I still cared about observing Sabbath at all, when it just felt like crossing t's and dotting i's.

I was taught, and I guess I *sort of* believed that the Sabbath was a day of rest. But I was feeling everything *but* rested on Sunday at 7pm. I was feeling stressed. Wrung out. Upset. Disappointed. You get the picture, and maybe you know it all too well. Where was all this promised rest and rejuvenation? Wherever it was, it was far, *far* away from me.

Sitting in my office one Saturday morning, I was dreading the next day. Even church seemed like a chore, wrestling kids into shoes, to the church pew, to the car, back home, and through the rest of the day, trapped in the house, watching it go from semi-clean to utter disaster before 3pm. Ugh. *"Not another Sunday"* I thought to myself.

My big office window faces the hillside that overlooks the whole Columbia Basin. It was foggy that morning, and the whole earth was covered in a soft blanket of clouds. I started doodling.

By now you know writing busies my hands so my mind can focus. My own version of meditation and prayer.

A thought came to me loud and clear. I pushed it away. Loud and clear, again it urged me to listen. Again, I pushed it away.

LOUD AND CLEAR, I heard the Spirit push me to stop and listen.

My heart was pounding, and my inner argument went something like this:

*"You need to get off your phone tomorrow for the whole day."*

*"Why? I'm not doing anything wrong."*

*"That doesn't matter."*

*"Sure, it does. I am not 'breaking the Sabbath' by being on my phone. It's a way to communicate. It's how I bring my scriptures to church. It's how I run my business. I share the Gospel through my phone on Sundays even."*

*"Put it away. **Put away the world and choose REST**."*

**I couldn't ignore this prompting.**

What started out as a *"yeah, okay, we'll see…"* turned into a full-on testimony of the Sabbath day.

That first Sunday was *hard*. Embarrassingly hard. Hard in a way I hate to admit. It was startling to see just how addicted I was to my phone in general, not just social media. I brought my actual scriptures to church, which were heavy and took up valuable space in my bag. I had to write down the month's events on a piece of torn paper instead of my calendar app. I missed a few texts and emails. I had to sit in silence and be with my thoughts. I was antsy for weather updates and notifications.

I began to not only see the impact social apps were on my Sabbath experience, but I also became aware of my addiction to busyness and noise in general. I noticed how difficult it was for me be *intentionally* **still.**

The Sabbath day was already set aside in my week, but simply crossing that t wasn't serving me. Which got me thinking, *was **Sabbath** ever supposed to serve **me**? Or was **I** actually supposed to serve a Sabbath?*

This idea shifted my mindset about what "observing Sabbath" truly meant.

*Why was I expecting a day of the week to produce some magical fairy dust of rest and worship and connectedness?* That actually makes no sense. It's a day in the week. But *me* serving a Sabbath, observing it for what it truly could be *through my own choices,* opened the door to a real, restful, and intentional day of worship.

Moving toward stillness outwardly with less technology and less world, initiated a higher way of worshiping on the Sabbath, with an inner stillness.

*"Be still, and know that I am God,"* (*Psalm 46:10, King James Version*).

Six days a week we are living by the sweat of our brow. Finding Sabbath, and an intentional inner stillness, created space to know God in a new and life-giving way.

There was still wrestling small children into church shoes, but, with a meditative inner stillness leading the way, I found the gift of presence, knowing, and rest, even in the thick of the regular drum beats of the day.

Turns out, I desperately needed a break from the world. I couldn't see it before I had it, I even scoffed at the inspiration from the Spirit, but the Lord knows what we need, even when we can't see it for ourselves.

Sabbath is a gift from Heavenly Parents who know how much we *need* rest from our labors, from our everyday rhythm of life six other days of the week. A rest from the constant flow of information and entertainment, a rest from the loud voices of the world.

I have found a pattern of worship each Sabbath that begins first thing in the morning and trickles into my week. I've found meaning in church attendance that goes beyond checking it off a list. My newfound inner stillness has brought a devotion to my Savior that strengthens my weaknesses and eases my burdens.

Guess what else I discovered? Everything I thought I was missing on Sunday was still there on Monday. The emails were there. The posts were there. The opportunities were there. It was all there.

But *I* was different when I resurfaced, and you will be too.

I was more capable of efficiently managing my time and attention. I was rested and ready to seek out the good and say #thanksbutnothanks to everything else. I was better focused on each *why* behind every *yes*.

I've said it before and I'll say it again here: you are not powerless to *anyone* or *anything*. You are a child of God, and while things may be messy, you've been sent *here* in this one and beautiful life. Right here, right now. The world only has as much power over your identity as you let it. The lies only become truth when you say so. Because as a child of the Highest, you have the power to overthrow **all** the lies the Adversary is trying so hard to sell you on. You have a literal connection with a Father in Heaven who loves you unconditionally, and a Savior who will go to bat for you again and again. You have the gift of the Holy Spirit that will show up, guide, and whisper to your heart what you need, even if you don't know it yet.

Find Sabbath and take back the rest only He can offer.

## AFFIRMATION:

I will find Sabbath on purpose. I will practice an intentional inner stillness through my own actions and choices and open my tired arms to the rest only He can grant. And He will.

_____

_____

_____

_____

_____

Who we choose to be in the waiting matters

♡ ⎯ ▽

# WAITING

## CHAPTER 20

One of my favorite Bible stories is found in John 5:1-30 (King James Version). It was believed that every so often an angel would stir the waters of the Pool of Bethesda, and the first one to enter would be healed from their infirmities. Oh, how many times I have wished for a magical pool within my own reach.

The book of John tells us there was a crippled man by the pool who had been carried to this sacred place, hoping to be healed by the magical waters. But in all the years he'd been there, had not been able to be first when the water stirred. Remaining a cripple, he continued to wait for his turn at the powerful waters.

Many of us suffer from things that don't seem fair. Maybe it's not you, but someone you love who is suffering. This particular man at the Pool of Bethesda, was believed to have been just a few steps from a life free of pain and physical limitation, and yet he did not receive that healing and deliverance.

I can't imagine the frustration and disappointment he felt at each opportunity for a miracle that passed him by.

I *know* that God is a God of miracles. I *know* He can heal and make whole the brokenness in us. But when we're *called to wait*, it's really hard to be patient with Him. It's no easy task to submit to God's will, surrendering our wants and desires for a humble *yes to all* that He puts on our path. In times of waiting, it can feel especially difficult to muster a *yes*, to *all*.

I've watched from a distance a young mom struggling to put her life back together after the loss of a daughter. The pangs of devastation never far away.

I have a younger brother who hasn't spoken to me in almost a decade. Birthday texts go unanswered year after year. I see photos of him and gasp--it's painful to have a brother that exists in the world without me. I don't know what he laughs at, where he lives, or what his days are like. I wait for reconciliation, but I hate this distance.

Maybe it's a broken relationship with a parent, years caught in limbo with no end in sight. Always wondering about their intentions and love.

Seasons of anxiety or depression, or both. Tight chests and worry as wide as the ocean, crippling fear and loud voices of worthlessness that never seem to let up.

A broken marriage with dark corners that desperately need to be unpacked. Words that need spoken. Feelings that need acknowledged. But it's never the right time, there's never enough space, there's never a good way.

Loss. Heartbreak. Cancer. Abandonment. Change. Abuse.

Seasons of painful waiting, all the same.

*If you are in a season of waiting, I love you. I see you. This fight right here is sacred ground. Don't give up. Keep walking. Keep trusting. Declare your yes, again and again.*

Jesus Christ comes to the pool of Bethesda and approaches this man, asking what he desires. The man shares his simple story: he desired to be healed by the pool's sacred powers, but with no one to carry him into the water when it moved, had been left a cripple for 38 years.

Without any special fanfare and without any magical waters, Christ tells the man to **get up and walk**. The man gets up and ***walks.***

He waited almost 40 years for this deliverance. I imagine that long season of suffering was filled with faith and doubt and all the feelings and emotions we feel in different, yet similar times of our own waiting. He was a human, after all.

But he waited nonetheless. He was patient. He surrendered his own timeline and his own desires to those of The Father. He remained diligent. *And he was healed.*

Of course, that's easier said than done.

It's hard to believe in miracles and still accept the will of God and His timing, plans, and purposes. It's easier to give in to the voice of the Adversary, who whispers that life is simply unfair, that no God would ever cause such pain and suffering in the world, in *your* world. It's easier to say *no* to "*this*" part of God's plan.

None of us will be spared from waiting in our suffering, sorrow, or affliction. It can be brutal, I know. But I'm learning every day *who* we choose to be in the waiting is what *really* matters.

The world wants us to be stuck on how unfair our circumstances seem at face value. It wants us to believe that we are not invited to God's miracles, when in fact His miracles were never a one-and-done type of deal. There was never a VIP guest list. He doesn't choose favorites. There is no A and B team. **He loves us each perfectly.**

Perhaps our most trying seasons are tailor made for us, *in* the waiting. Maybe the waiting is the whole point. Maybe *in* the wait we learn something about God that we couldn't learn otherwise.

There's a story in Mark (King James Version) right in the thick of Jesus' healings and miracles. Jairus comes to Jesus wrecked with grief because his daughter had just died. Jairus pleads with Jesus to come to his home and bring his daughter back, but is met with the devastating response from the other apostles not to trouble the Master about it, for she was already passed.

*Have you ever felt that no matter how many times you've knocked on God's door, no one seems to be home? Struggling so deep you're sure you'll never find rest again?*

Listen to me: **fear is a liar.**

When the tough stuff comes, we always, always, *always,* have a choice. *Do we allow fear to cripple us spiritually, or do we instead* **choose yes to faith, anyway?**

Jesus responded to Jairus, *"Be not afraid, only believe."* Then He travels to his house and brings his 12-year-old daughter back to life.

Maybe waiting through seasons of disappointments, struggles, anxieties, and on and on, make renewing our strength on the Lord uniquely *empowering*. Maybe waiting as the underdog, underappreciated, lonely, or fearful makes freedom from those struggles as free as an eagle soaring over the earth.

Maybe, after the wait by the edge of the pool, Christ's quiet and powerful redemption for the enduring man, is *everything*.

*"The Spirit of the Lord is upon me, because he hath anointed me to preach the gospel to the poor; he hath sent me to heal the brokenhearted, to preach deliverance to the captives, recovering of sight to the blind, to set at liberty them that are bruised," (Luke 4:18, King James Version).*

*Why do you think God speaks sight to the blind, healing to the broken, and deliverance to the captive?*

I am learning that each season of waiting, restlessness, and struggle are tailor made for my *own* personal growth. I'm beginning to see that deliverance is only truly appreciated by the captive, sight miraculous to the blind, and healing intensely powerful to the broken. God meets us *where we are* when we choose *yes* to faith no matter what.

Captive? He delivers. Blind? He restores sight. Broken? He heals. And only after waiting in captivity, blindness, and brokenness, can we learn to close the door on fear and believe in His power and timing instead.

Those moments transform us into rooted and faithful disciples of Christ. They set something into motion that no storm can stop.

*What if there is no end to the waiting? What if the waiting is our earthly experience?*

In Daniel 3 (New International Version), Shadrach, Meshach and Abednego are cast into a burning furnace for their personal belief in God. They express their confidence in His deliverance boldly and courageously.

They are prepared to wait on the Lord. They declare a brave *yes* to even *this.*

**"But even if he does not,** *we want you to know, Your Majesty, that we will not serve your gods or worship the image of gold you have set up,"* *(Daniel 3:18, New International Version).*

**But if not,** we will **not** stop believing and having faith and trust in a delivering and loving God.

Perhaps, *in* the waiting we come to know God, we come to know deliverance, we come to know Jesus. Perhaps, *in* the waiting we are molded and refined into His steadfast sheep. Committed and wildly faithful, even to the bitter end.

No matter what.

## AFFIRMATION:

I will have patience, faith, trust, and hope even in my own personal wait on God. I am His. There is no circumstance that is not known by Him. There is no earthly circumstance that I cannot see through to the end. I will choose *yes* to my God, for He is a God of miracles, love, and deliverance. Always

Yes to faith, no matter what.

♡ ◻ ⊽

# SUNFLOWERS

## CHAPTER 21

This year a farmer down the road from our home planted a whole field of sunflowers. They started as tiny seeds and then pushed through the dirt showing off their bright green leaves. Facing the sun, they got taller and bloomed, and the whole field was a bright yellow.

Their beauty was disarming. But they only lasted a few weeks before their heavy heads began to droop, their bright yellow beauty turning brown from head to toe. This is the life of a sunflower. They grow to produce tiny seeds to make more beauty. From one flower hundreds more get to be. The dying of the sunflower *is* the point. In fact, they're left in rows until they're fully dried up.

I drove by the other day and noticed the farmer had put out scarecrows since the flowers had begun this new season of dying.

I thought, *why now? Why not protect them from birds when they're in their full bloom state? Why would the birds suddenly be interested now that they're void of life?*

The birds don't pick on them when they're standing tall, they come when they're drooping.

*And so it goes with us, doesn't it?*

We all have seasons in life when we too are standing tall, disarmingly confident and sure. Facing the sun and shining so brightly. But there's no stopping the sunsets and sunrises, August gives way to September, spring, summer, fall and winter. We too experience seasons like the once radiant rows of sunflowers—seasons of shadow, sinking, and change.

When we're there, in the thick of it, is when the crows always seem to show up.

*What are the crows in your life?*

For me, seasons that compel me to slow down, seem to chip away at my worth or value. At times I'm troubled with anxiety and depression, worry and anger. I struggle to wait in my current circumstances, not knowing what the next season will hold. By now you know my inner demons well. I am learning that while the specifics of our individual seasons of uphill mountain climbing may look totally different, but our experience of them are so much the same.

I wonder as I drive by, *why not harvest the sunflowers now? Why put the crop through another day of pestering birds?*

Have you ever felt the same way in your own life? I have. In fact, those thoughts play on repeat when I'm in seasons of transition for longer than I'd like.

*How many more days will I have to spend in bed?* I ask God daily, sick and with a growing baby in my womb. *How much longer will cancer plague my brother?* I pray day in and day out. *How much more can a marriage handle? How many more sleepless nights? How many more sick days for this baby?* I beg for health. *How much more can I take?* I pray for strength.

*How much longer?!* I ask God. And it's not a rhetorical question. I really want to know. In fact, I'm more or less demanding an answer from Him. However, I'm learning we can't rush a day, month, or season. It will last as long as it lasts. I've yet to see a sunflower uproot itself and take off.

*"I'm done!"* said no sunflower ever.

If there's one thing I've learned about farming, it's that you harvest when it's time, and you don't when it's not.

Watching the sunflowers, now weeks into being ruthlessly attacked by birds hungry for their hard-earned seeds, they consistently stand *still* and *endure*. I am reminded that though the yellow has long since turned to brown, their worth is not one bit less.

The farmer will harvest those flowers and the value is not in their flashy petals at all. The value is in the outcome of this *exact* season. The once shining flowers with white and green middles have given way to black seeds and crispy leaves. And *now* they are at their *full potential.* Now they are harvestable. Now they are perfect.

The days between yellow and brown are sacred time in a sunflower's life. It transforms them into what they were *created to become.* It *pushes* them to reach their full potential. They stand still and quite literally, *lean* into the transformation.

I'm learning that the seasons *between* thinking "I can take on the world" are where I become who I was created to be. The moments of total reliance on Heavenly help to get up and continue onward are what refine us in a million ways. The walk, in absolute faith with no vision for what's ahead while the crows pester, is what binds us to our Heavenly Parents, who **know** and **love.** The hope in tomorrow when today is never ending, stretches our capacity for such a wild thing as hope, at all.

You know what I didn't witness as I watched the field of sunflowers day after day? I didn't see them fight against the brown, the drooping, or even the pecking crows. They *became,* right there in the thick of it.

I am no expert on anything. In fact, if you lived inside our four walls, you'd know that I am very far from any such thing. I have made it a habit over my 30+ years on this earth to make a mess of things, and often.

I'm learning though, in life, and in all the sacred seasons we weather, we make mistakes and *become* transformed *through* them. It's climbing up mountains, and battling on the front lines of all our individual and tailor-made struggles, waiting to someday stand firm as who God intended us to be.

We need to create more intentional space to be seen by God, more courage to stand firm where He calls us to stand, and more faith, no matter what the circumstances may hold, or questions that rush to the surface. More trust that His plans are higher than ours. More confidence that His ways are intentionally designed to push us to truly *become* all that he created us to be.

Struggling to understand the intricate details of this purposeful plan God had for me as His daughter, I got a sitter and met Tyler at the temple. I'd cried for hours the day before, and just needed a moment of peace.

Sitting in a sacred place, dressed in white, I deeply pondered and prayed for clarity.

No angel appeared, no miracle seen by the world happened, I didn't receive perfect vision of the future, or an essay on the meaning of life.

Instead I *felt* better. I *felt* known. I *felt* seen. I *felt* loved.

And from there, I was taught through the Spirit of God, the sacred reality, that while we may drive by a field of dying sunflowers and wonder *"why,"* **He has a plan, and it's always plan A.** There is no plan B, not for me, you, or them. Not for sunflowers or our human lives. Everything is just as it is supposed to be. Just because individually, in a marriage, relationship, or circumstance we wonder *why* the clouds loom or darkness consumes, does not mean that God's not working above it all.

He is.

Read it again: **HE IS.**

The powerful reality that you are loved now, then, and tomorrow is a beautiful witness that even if the crows circle, the yellow fades, and your heart aches, in due time, you too will *become.*

If a field of sunflowers can stand still and lean in through all seasons, so can I.

And so, can *you.*

You are Loved

# *L*OVED

## CHAPTER 22

Learning that I am loved perfectly, opened the door to saying *yes* to it *all* with relentless faith.

*"I love them that love me; and those that seek me early shall find me,"* (*Proverbs 8:17, King James Version*).

*What makes you question God's love for you?*

I want to offer that each of those reasons, big or small, are *irrelevant* when it comes to the love of perfect Heavenly Parents. That may seem harsh right off the cuff. I know, because if you had said that to me a few years ago I would've felt defensive about all my own reasons why *I* wasn't loved. They were real to me. They were even significant defining factors in who I believed I was to my core. All the evidence I had collected over a lifetime of mistakes, struggle, guilt, and shame made me who I was, and I was sure I did not deserve divine love.

But here's the thing, all of our carefully collected evidence of any such thing, is a *lie*. The Adversary glories in those false beliefs. He uses them against us over and over like a broken record, spinning us into a web of reasons as to why we are not worthy of love. He'll do this until we are convinced it's the truth.

I pray that you decide to choose *yes* to being loved, and *no* to the lies of the Adversary. It's not going to be easy. In fact, he will attack from all sides and work to twist you up into knots, desperate to keep you from a divine love like you've never known. Choosing *yes* to being loved is a daily practice of retraining your heart and mind on Jesus and a Father who doesn't yell and shout, but whispers through the storm instead.

Even after all I had done to come back to the narrow path of faith and trust and asking and seeking, stubbornly insisting that I was the exception to the rule when it came to my Heavenly Parent's love, was stopping me from seeing my own potential. And not just in the big picture stuff, but in the small daily moments too.

Continually seeking God in a million little ways, each day, slowly but surely uncovered the truth that rocked my world. **I am loved.** I am loved wholly, right where I stand. There isn't an "if" or "but" attached to His love. It just IS, because *I* am His daughter. **End of story**.

Once I bravely said *yes*, His love has been the solid ground when everything else feels unstable. It has centered and grounded me, even when the claws of the Adversary threaten to destroy me.

Embracing and choosing *yes* to your own belovedness will do the same for you. I pray you walk away from this book with the unwavering truth written on your heart: **YOU ARE LOVED.**

## AFFIRMATION:

I will boldly choose *no* to any and all lies the Adversary will whisper to my heart and mind, and choose *yes* to the truth that **I am loved.** **Loved** by Heavenly Parents who know me, my struggles, my joys, my heart, and true self. **I am loved** and heard and cherished. I am not alone in this life. **I am loved** now, as I am, where I stand.

_____

_____

_____

_____

_____

_____

_____

_____

_____

_____

_____

_____

_____

_____

_____

_____

_____

_____

You are
KNOWN
you are
HEARD
you are
FOUND
you are
LOVED

♡ ⚬ ▽

# SEA·CHANGE

## CHAPTER 23

*Sea-change: a profound transformation.*

I feel like I've spent the last decade of my life in a constant state of personal change.

Standing in this place, I can see how each bump and twist in the road has played a pivotal role in the sea-change of self. Who I chose to be yesterday directly impacts who I am today. Choices to nourish my whole self, mind body and soul today directly impact who I am tomorrow. Each day, each *yes* to faith and trust and hope, lacing together, profoundly transforming who I am, into who I can be.

*Becoming*, every day.

The sea-change and godly transformation that happens with each *yes* to God creates our conversion. That heart and soul change was never designed to be a one time, check it off, finish line kind of journey. There *is no* finish line. There is no race. There is no winning. And there is no losing.

Our conversion is the daily, slow and steady process of choosing *yes* again and again.

*Will we have perfect yeses across the board?*

No.

*Is faith only worth working toward if it can be a perfect faith?*

I'm coming to believe that striving for perfection in faith is not the point. In fact, I'm learning that instead of perfection from me, God expects something different, something *higher.*

*"Thou shalt be perfect **with** the Lord thy God,"* (*Deuteronomy* 18:13, *King James Version*).

This verse doesn't say, "Thou shalt be perfect *for* the Lord thy God." It says *"with* the Lord." There's a big difference.

Your one and only life is not a performance. It is not a marathon. It's not a pageant. Your one and only, beautifully messy life, is a walk *with* God. *Through it all.* With your falters and failures and fears. Through the ups and downs, your faith and conversion to your Father in Heaven is not a prize at the end of a human existence, it's right here and now.

And your conversion does not require perfection.

Find me one person in all of scripture that had perfect faith, with a perfect *yes* to every single circumstance God called them to. Find me one person in your life or throughout the history of time that walked a perfect road, with a perfect faith, in perfect harmony with God's will. There was only One, and his name was Jesus.

If God is who He says He is, if Jesus Christ is who he came to earth to be, then you my friend, do not need to be perfect at any of this. God is love. Jesus is grace and redemption, and those gifts are for *you*, today and every day after.

"*God dwelleth in us, and his love is **perfected** in us*," (1 John 4:12,17-18, New International Version).

His love is perfected *in* us. *What does that mean to you?*

When I think of Him as a Father, I long for that kind of perfect love for my own children. But I am not God. I am Courtney, an imperfect mom trying my best to love my imperfect children. I love them, but I yell and mess up. I try, but I am still far from perfection in motherhood.

*Does that mean I'm an unfit mother? That I should walk away from motherhood altogether?*

No, of course not.

*If we're imperfect in marriage, does that warrant ending it completely?*

Not in the slightest.

*If we never make it to the Olympics and win gold, does that mean we should never run or jump or ski?*

No. It does not.

**God is perfect *in* us.** The very existence of our struggles perfects His love.

Your daily *yes* to God and a faith that knows no bounds, will protect and provide through all seasons. It will ground you in a world that wants nothing more than to scatter and destroy you.

Here's the deal, you were perfectly made, and that *includes* all those imperfections. You were placed right where you are, whether you stumbled there, ran there, or were thrown there by circumstances outside of your control. You are in the hands of your Father, and while you will not walk a perfect path, with perfect faith, making perfect choices, you are *still* held and known and loved. Your efforts toward *yes* in faith and trust and seeking and finding *matter*. The ebbs and flows in your faith are part of His plan, if not the key piece to it. The ebbs create the flows. The flows allow the ebbs. *And it's all okay.*

*"Yea, come unto Christ, and be perfected **in him**, and deny yourselves of all ungodliness; and if ye shall deny yourselves of all ungodliness, and **love God with all your might, mind and strength, then is his grace sufficient for you**, that by his grace ye may be perfect **in** Christ; and if by the grace of God ye are **perfect in Christ**, ye can in nowise deny the power of God,"* (Moroni 10:32-33, *The Book of Mormon*).

Your own personal conversion will be a constant *sea-change*, a profound change that alters everything, one *yes* at a time, like the waves of the sea repeatedly crashing on the shore over and over again.

The process of conversion is a lifelong process and that path is sacred ground, a winding road with twists and turns heavy with mistakes and detours, but also endless grace and love.

♡ ◯ ◁

# MORE than AIR

## CHAPTER 24

In May of 2006, a mudslide sloughed off a large portion of the bluff that we live on. The slide did serious damage to the main road going through the area, blocking it completely, making it totally unusable.

This was a huge deal in our small community I'm told, and took over 6 months just to figure out what to do next, let alone the long-time construction process to create a completely new Road 170.

The impact of a road closure like this is hard to understand, unless your kids have ever had an hour bus route to and from kindergarten. Getting from point A to point B, already quite the process, this slide was more than just an inconvenience, it was devastating to many. Even when plans of the new road started to be discussed, the impact on farmers was a serious consideration, as it would deem acres and acres unusable for their livelihood.

I wasn't living here then, but I've seen photos of our bluffs post slide. It was ugly. It was scary. It was unfathomable, until you realize, it is fathomable. It happened. It's right there.

At the end of a slightly uphill road leading to the slide, is a road closed sign. The yellow lines and pavement keep going a little further, until you can't see them anymore.

What was a huge loss to a small farming community, is now a beautiful, lush, forest like place, in the middle of a sagebrush-covered hillside. As a family we've hiked all around up in the slide, and it's an amazing little pocket right beneath our home. There are wild animals living there, and large ponds filled with giant frogs. Green deciduous trees with changing color leaves and dusty trails for hiking or four wheeling.

That road is sort of a sacred pocket for me. One that I don't talk about often, because it's just a road, I know. I started walking it daily, sometimes twice a day, during a year that altered the entire course of my life. The year when I wrestled with *yes* and *no* like my life depended on it. The year before all this choosing faith stuff started. **The year of dabbling in darkness and fighting for faith.**

I would walk, or ran, and demand God's promises over my life.

*"I can do **all** things through Christ that strengthens me! He is **my** Savior; I* **can** *do this **with** Him! His Atonement **will** heal me! I **will** be made whole. I **can** do this!"*

Over and over again.

I walked and ran thousands of steps on that road. Sometimes alone. Sometimes with a friend. All the time grasping at small inklings of light and glimmers of hope. Sometimes speaking my fears and questions aloud. Sometimes, unable to continue on, collapsing at the end, surrendering to the confusion and tears and devastation, next to that old, beat up, road closed sign.

I guess this is how I was supposed to come to know my Savior. How I was to find my own unwavering *yes,* to God. **I needed a rescuer, more than I needed oxygen**. And because of that intoxicating need, I would be stopped at nothing, to be found by Him.

Your way there will look different.

But we all have to find our way there. We have to uncover a *"why"* to our conversion and faith and hope, somehow. We have to *need* it and *want* it so badly; nothing can stop us from getting there.

I could go through any person's story in all of scripture, and the ones who remained faithful to the end had a *why* that was so big and brave and absolute, they simply could not be moved.

When life seems past fixing, past hope, I'm here to tell you with every ounce of my heart and soul, *that is not so.*

Whenever I'm up at the hill slide, and I try to spend quiet moments there often, I am tenderly reminded of the goodness of God and the ways that *he makes all things **new.***

The mud slide was awful. It was devastating. And it never got fixed. They never brought in giant equipment to remove the mud and reopen the road.

Years and years and years have passed, and what was a small-town tragedy now is a pocket of new life found in a totally unexpected place.

Our Father in Heaven, in His infinite love and compassion on you and me, makes all things new. Our lives, our hearts, souls, our whole selves. *In time*, He breathes new life into even our most demolished places, when we move in a *yes* toward Him.

You don't need to travel to Bali to find yourself; you don't need to tackle every single question or doubt or fear right this very second. You don't need to read the entire Bible this year. You don't need to have perfect attendance at church for 30 days. You don't need to address every wound and every heartache all at once. You don't need to spend 16 hours on your knees in prayer.

You really just need to first; decide *why* you **need** a *yes* to God. And when you find it, you'll know. It has probably surfaced more than once as you've read this book. *What made your heart stir? What brought quiet tears to the surface? What made you close it, because it felt too confronting or raw? Why do you need a **yes** to faith? Why do you need a **yes** to hope? Why do you need a **yes** to Jesus?* **More than air, more than anything.**

Once you have found your *why*, you declare your *yes* to His *all*, and keep it at the helm of everything else, moving in obedience, once step and another and another.

Every day, getting back on that narrow and less traveled road. Speaking or whispering or demanding God's promises over your life. Again, and again.

If I could say it any louder or clearer or with more vigor, I would.

Hold on. Don't give up. Keep walking, keep trusting, and keep *choosing yes*, to it *all*.

You are known.

You are heard.

***You are loved.***

You are
Loved

# ACKNOWLEDGEMENTS

So much love to those of you who have been in my corner since day one of Courtney Casper Letters, and to the even more of you who have joined the party along the way. The internet is a strange place, but I personally have found so much goodness there, so much friendship, so much encouragement and so much humanity. That's 100% thanks to you. I'm humbled to be among you as sisters in His Kingdom.

Special thanks to Christin Ricks, Angelee Hope, Jessica Pickett, Hana Dodd, Stephanie Joyner, Crissy Boss, and Annie Ditto for offering their time and insight in my beta reader groups. I know those first few read-throughs were not easy, but you trudged through anyway. And truthfully this book wouldn't be anything close to what it is without your love and help. THANK YOUUUU!

Many thanks to my friend Kayla Geddes for also doubling as my first-round editor. I'm kinda really excited for you to read this version, so you can see how far it's come! ;)

Special thanks to Phil Davis at Alphagraphics who told me a few years ago that I was a successful self-published author. It was the first time someone other than my inner circle had allowed me to be what I secretly hoped I was. He validated the hard work and learning and growth that I wanted to downplay, and I'll be forever thankful for that. Alphagraphics in Lehi, Utah is hands down the best printer around! ;)

All my love to the few women that come together on snowy September days in corner booths to share their truth and struggles and hearts. Women who snuggle sick babies, fold laundry, cheer you on, walk closed roads in the dark, and let you whisper secrets in passenger seats, never telling a soul. Women who will be in your corner through thick and thin, willing to hold the heavy stuff with you when you just can't anymore. You are my people, and I love you.

I know he will absolutely not approve of this but I'm his big sister so I do what I want. Thank you, Jake, for teaching me so much about resiliency and getting up and getting on with life even when it sucks. Even when you don't want to. Even when you're tired, sick, and disappointed, again. Thank you for teaching me to rely on even the ONE thing you DO know when you're unsure about everything else. Thank you for snuggling my babies and making my kids laugh for hours on end. Thank you for teaching me so much about true health and wellness and meditation. Thank you for teaching me that it's okay to feel our feelings, as long as we get up and go to Iceland too. I love you Jake. Since day one of your life, and forever and ever.

I wouldn't be me without my mom. I could fill this whole page as a tribute to you, but I'll just say this: thank you for fighting for me, every day of my life. I'm standing here, in part, because you wouldn't allow it to be any other way. I think I get my stubbornness from you, and I'm thankful for that.

And the very biggest thank you to my husband and children. I'm not always very good at balancing everything, so thank you for showing me endless amounts of grace when I make mistakes and mess up. *Tyler,* there are never enough words that I could type that could possibly express what you mean to me. You are my soulmate and I choose you again and again. Wow. Gushy, I know! But it's the truth.

My girls! *Lynley,* thank you for inspiring me in all things. You are going to do amazing things in this life, and I am honored to get a front row seat as your mom.

*Callie,* never lose your vulnerability and tenderness, my girl. And please, always snuggle up on my lap. Yes, even when you're twenty. ;)

*Elaine!* My "kind of" baby. You've seen the most of the last few years, and the writing of this book and ministry and finding of self. Through it all you've been such a constant force for love. Never lose that fierce loving drive! It's a gift.

And, last but not least, baby *Nolan* boy. You are the rainbow after the storm. A gift that no one will ever know the depth of, but your dad and me. I just wish you could keep those cheeks forever and ever!

Look
FiND
cHoose

COURTNEY CASPER

FAITH
hope
& trust
are all a
CHOICE

He
is
Here

COURTNEY CASPER

Yes to faith, no matter what.

COURTNEY CASPER

You are
KNOWN
you are
HEARD
you are
FOUND
you are
LOVED

COURTNEY CASPER

Courtneycasper.com
Courtneycasper.letters@gmail.com
@courtneycasper.letters